Praise for *Writing Toward Wholeness*, Susan M. Tiberghien

Maureen Murdock

In *"Writing Toward Wholeness"* Tiberghien gives the reader access to Jung's inner thoughts as he dialogued with his Soul in his journals. She encourages us to do likewise by developing a relationship with our Soul by following the image it presents to us. In so doing, journaling becomes a spiritual practice. Calling upon the writings of such spiritual elders as Hildegaard of Bingen, Etty Hillesum, Thomas Merton and Annie Dillard, Tiberghien shows us how to write toward wholeness as we engage this "silent place of the spirit." A deeply nurturing and inspiring book.
—Maureen Murdock, Ph.D., Author of *The Heroine's Journey: Women's Quest for Wholeness*

Wallis Wilde-Menozzi

In *Writing Toward Wholeness,* Susan Tiberghien distills a lifetime of prayerful attention. Using Carl Jung's journey, above all in *the Red Book,* she traces possibilities each of us has for a rounder, more conscious existence. A gifted teacher, she shows how creative energies are within our grasp and how writing practice can be part of spiritual growth.
—Wallis Wilde-Menozzi, Poet and Author of *Mother Tongue*

James Hollis

The most interesting conversation we ever have may prove to be with our own depths. Rather than narcissistic self-absorption, through this dialogue something within responds, speaks back to us, and out of that unfolding conversation we begin to discover, engage, and assimilate unknown parts of ourselves. As a template for this summons toward greater wholeness, Susan Tiberghien's *Writing Toward Wholeness* provides examples of how other thoughtful people deepened their journey, as well as a host of questions and exercises which stir and stimulate our own conversation with the soul.
—James Hollis, Ph.D., Jungian Analyst in Washington D.C. and Author of numerous books

Paul Pearson

In *Writing Toward Wholeness* Susan Tiberghien profoundly calls us to experience what Thomas Merton called the "hidden wholeness," the "hidden ground of love," within our deepest selves. This volume invites us to take up our pen and to journal, guiding us, chapter by chapter, as we create our own path to our true self.
—Paul M. Pearson, Ph.D., Director, Thomas Merton Center

Kristina Schellinki

Writing towards Wholeness invites to an encounter with self. Susan Tiberghien is not just *showing* the reader a way towards at-one-ness in the light of creation; she is *creating* such a path by her writing. Those seeking their own path towards wholeness can open these pages and will find sparks of inspiration from ancient and modern texts as well as from Susan's international teaching experience which has led countless participants of her workshops to become successful authors. Susan loves *and* creates *and* lives through writing. Like Carl Gustav Jung and Thomas Merton, this author has found wholeness and so will the reader inspired by her writing. It is the "path of a lifetime."
—Kristina Schellinski, Jungian Analyst, Geneva, Switzerland

Robert Hinshaw

In this reflective work on the virtues of writing, Susan Tiberghien encourages the reader with excerpts from Jung, the world of Zen and her own considerable life experience. The Writing toward Wholeness journey is richly accompanied by images from Jung's *Red Book* and other inspired sources, along with helpful exercises. In the course of recording our dreams, visions and imaginations, we both anticipate and honor our destiny.
—Robert Hinshaw, Ph.D., Faculty, C.G. Jung Institute of Zurich, Publisher, Daimon Verlag

Writing Toward Wholeness

Lessons Inspired by C.G. Jung

Susan M. Tiberghien

CHIRON PUBLICATIONS • ASHEVILLE, NORTH CAROLINA

www.ChironPublications.com

Cover photo, Chapelle des Macchabées, Cathédrale St. Pierre, Geneva, Switzerland, Susan Tiberghien
Interior and cover design by Danijela Mijailović
Printed primarily in the United States of America.

ISBN 978-1-63051-454-9 paperback
ISBN 978-1-63051-455-6 hardcover
ISBN 978-1-63051-456-3 electronic
ISBN 978-1-63051-457-0 limited edition paperback

Library of Congress Cataloging-in-Publication Data Pending

Contents

Foreword 9

Introduction 13

1. Keeping Your Own Red Books: Writing to the Soul 15

2. Pursuing Images: Active Imagination 37

3. Exploring Dreams: Listening and Writing 61

4. Composing Metaphor: Illuminating Lives 85

5. Seeing Beauty with Words: Awakening the Soul 109

6. Practicing Alchemy: From Darkness to Light 133

7. Learning Zen: Clear Seeing, Clear Writing 159

8. Writing Toward Wholeness: Cultivating the Self 187

Bibliography 217

Credits 221

Index 225

About the Author 231

Illustrations and Credits

The Red Book, C.G. Jung, Photo, Susan Tiberghien   17

My Journal, Photo, Susan Tiberghien   26

White Forsythia in Winter, Photo, Susan Tiberghien   34

Tree Bending Down, Journal Drawing,   49
Susan Tiberghien

My Soul Approached Me, C.G. Jung, Image 107,   52
The Red Book
W.W. Norton & Company, Inc.*

Dogwood Blossom, Journal Drawing,   54
Susan Tiberghien

Window to Eternity, C.G. Jung, Image 159,   69
The Red Book
W.W. Norton & Company, Inc.*

Green Frog from China, Photo, Susan Tiberghien   75

Cultivating the Cosmic Tree, Hildegard of Bingen   92
© Photo Scala, Florence**

Rhizome, Journal Drawing, Susan Tiberghien   95

Crack in the Water Jug, Photo, Susan Tiberghien   105

Night Sinks Blue, C.G. Jung, Image 131,   121
The Red Book
W.W. Norton & Company, Inc.*

Labyrinth at Chartres Cathedral, Drawing,   124
Public Domain

The Way of Evergreen Ivy, Photo, Susan Tiberghien   131

Alchemists at Work, 18th century manuscript   138
Manuscript: Motus Liber 1702, Mellon Collection.***

The Philosopher's Stone, C.G. Jung, Image 121,   147
The Red Book
W.W. Norton & Company, Inc.*

Cinquefoil, Photo, Susan Tiberghien   154

Double Buttercup, Photo, Susan Tiberghien   155

Master and Disciple, The Way of Chuang Tzu   161
The Mustard Seed Garden Manual, Public Domain

Blossoming Ginkgo Tree, Photo, Susan Tiberghien   170

Doorway to the Sea, the Tower at Bollingen,   175
Photo Susan Tiberghien

Systema munditotius, C.G. Jung, The Red Book   195
© 2007 Foundation of the Works of C.G. Jung,
Zürich, and with permission of Robert Hinshaw

The Tower at Bollingen, Photo © cgjung.net   203

Sophia, Thomas Merton, Drawing   207
Used with permission of the Merton Legacy Trust and
the Thomas Merton Center at Bellarmine University

Acknowledgements

Writing Toward Wholeness is the fruit of over 30 years of Jungian reading and reflection. It was a Jungian Catholic priest, Richard Frost, now deceased, who reawakened my interest in the work of C.G. Jung, back in the 1980s here in Geneva. Two friends, Christina Ekeus-Oldfelt and Kristina Schellinski, inspired me to delve deeper. I entered analysis with Keller, a Swiss analyst, whom I thank for our years together. My Jungian path continued, and I acknowledge all those who have encouraged me along the way. I especially thank Robert Hinshaw in Einsiedeln, the editor of my first book, *Looking for Gold, A Year in Jungian Analysis*, in 1995. There follows the many Jungians who invited me to their different societies and institutes across the States and in Switzerland. These workshops and lectures are the groundwork of *Writing Toward Wholeness*. Without the support of these people and still others who have made me listen to echoes of Jung's voice, there would be no book.

This brings me to all that I owe to the writers who have been at my side for these many years. I particularly wish to thank one writer friend, Wallis Wilde-Menozzi, author and poet, who over the years has given me precious counsel on my work, including this manuscript. I am grateful to all those in the International Women's Writing Guild and in the Geneva Writers' Group who have accompanied and encouraged me on this journey. Then there are the many authors whom I have cited in this book and whose work I continue to appreciate. I thank them for the short excerpts of their work which I have included on these pages.

7

The subject "writing toward wholeness" encompasses not only Jungians and writers but also spiritual teachers. I acknowledge here the person, who alongside of C.G. Jung has been a mentor for over 50 years, the Trappist monk Thomas Merton. His work has helped me see "the hidden wholeness" of creation.

I would like to express my deep appreciation to Chiron Publications and to my editor, Jennifer Fitzgerald, who believed in this book and brought it to life. It continues to be a joy to work together.

To conclude, I thank my husband, Pierre-Yves—the Frenchman I fell in love with at Grenoble University some 60 odd years ago—who listens, reads my work, and pushes me forward with his questions and still more with his amazing love. I thank also my six children, their spouses, and my 16 grandchildren who give me hope and trust in the future of our world.

Foreword
Murray Stein

Keeping a journal is a method for keeping track of the ebb and flow of consciousness within the stream of time. Life refuses to remain still, and our memory of subtle details is fragmentary and evanescent. When you look back over so many years, as I do now in my eighth decade, the view is impressionistic at best with a few salient details scattered here and there across the vast landscape. If you keep a journal, however, you can retrieve the intricate detail of specific experiences, whether they be dreams, feelings, thoughts, or encounters with other people. This book, *Writing Toward Wholeness*, will help you give much better coverage to your inner life.

William James writes about consciousness as a stream. The stream has fringes that melt into the depths of the unknown and disappear into the darkness of the unconscious. If you study the fringes, you will find many surprises. Hermes lives at the edge of consciousness. Mysteries lie there. These are potential treasures, but only if you pick them up and hold on to them. The god is in the details. Write them down!

The author of this fine book, Susan Tiberghien, encourages you not only to keep a journal of daily happenings and activities, but to look carefully to the dim edge of consciousness and record what you see there. This means paying scrupulous attention to those random and fleeting feelings that look like mist on the morning river, to the dim associations to encounters and impressions that give you joy or a bellyache, and to note meaningful coincidences that come across your path by surprise. In retrospect, these will tell you a lot about your psychic constitution and about the subtle nuances of experience that taken together and raised into consciousness will add up to a distinct sense of meaning. The author gives you inspiring examples of this.

Writing calls you to attention. It is a discipline, and it sharpens your observations. Coming home after a cocktail party, go to your desk and record if you can what you saw, who said what, who was absent, the décor of the rooms occupied, the mood of the room and the people gathered there, and then go a step further and record what you were thinking as you interacted with friends or strangers, how you felt, what memories came to your mind, and what surprising coinciden-ces you noticed between what you were thinking quietly and what other people were saying and doing. If you want to read a brilliant example of such observations committed to paper, go to Marcel Proust. He was the master.

It is noteworthy that when C.G. Jung calls out in the night to his soul, "Where are you?" at the beginning of his midlife journal, *The Red Book*, he notes that it has been twelve 12 years since he was last in contact with "her." The editor of *The Red Book* tells us in a footnote that this corresponds to when Jung had left off writing in his journal, the so-called "black books." There is something about a journal that keeps the soul nearby, that keeps communication live and flowing between the surface of consciousness and the depths of psyche, by the act of writing. Writing in this particular way one might call deep writing.

This is what is advocated in the book you are opening. The author is sharing her experience of writing for soul and offering practical lessons in how you may follow in this discipline. Does it build toward wholeness? Yes. And this is because this type of writing brings into play the deeper levels of awareness by focusing on the fringes of consciousness, by gathering associations and memories, by weaving a fabric of psyche that includes conscious and unconscious material. This deepens a person toward the inherent wholeness that lies within.

Freud's greatest book, *The Interpretation of Dreams*, is an example of this type of writing. Most of the dreams recorded there are his, and the method he uses to interpret them is free association. Take a figure and associate to it. Where does this lead? Before you know it, you have discovered something previously only vaguely intuited, something that lies at the fringe of consciousness. Take it further, and it will reveal something truly hidden away from your daily view of yourself. This is the essence of psychoanalysis. This is an exploration of psyche in words.

Any person can benefit from keeping a journal of experiences, dreams, associations, and feelings. This is not for the purpose of becoming a masterful author like Marcel Proust any more than making sketches or paintings of your dreams has the purpose of becoming another Rembrandt or Picasso. This project is for self-knowledge, not for career. Keeping a journal is communion with your soul. This is its purpose, this is its meaning. The elaboration of subjectivity in words on the page is equivalent to growing into the body you were destined to have by virtue of your genetic constitution. We write in a journal to become and to know who we are, not to tell what we already know. The audience is internal. The matter is soul.

I have studied Jung's *Red Book* quite intensively over the past several years. It is an account of his encounter with himself in words and images. He tells us years later that this was the major turning point in his adult life, from which flowed many of his later ideas and works, as well as novel

11

methods and techniques for making contact with the psyche in depth. He undertook a risky venture and survived. For us, the risks are not so great because we have his story of the journey as a support. His greatest discovery was the inner world, and this is a territory that we too can explore by using the method of active imagination and recording our experiences. The journey inward is an adventure in discovery. What is discovered by those who go this way are symbols that are alive and shine with numinous power and intensity. These will form the foundation for a personal myth to live by. As Jesus said of the kingdom of God, this is a treasure which neither moths nor rust doth corrupt. It is our eternal home.

Wholeness is not some esoteric notion. It is down-to-earth, immediate, lived experience. And it is available to anyone who takes the time and gives the energy to delve into the inner world of psyche. Keeping a journal is a method for pursuing this adventure, and this work by Susan Tiberghien is a helpful, enlightening guide.

Murray Stein, Ph.D. is a Jungian psychoanalyst practicing in Zurich, Switzerland and a training and supervising analyst at the International School of Analytical Psychology in Zurich (ISAPZurich). He is the author of numerous books, including *Jung's Map of the Soul* and *Outside Inside and All Around.*

Introduction

It was after my forum lecture at the C.G. Jung Foundation in New York City in May 2015 that I was asked if the text for my lecture, "Writing Toward Wholeness," was available. I replied no, that I spoke from my notes. However, the question stayed in my mind, and within a few months, I had an outline for this book. I would title it *Writing Toward Wholeness*, and it would include many of the subjects I have been presenting at different Jung Societies and Institutes over more than 15 years, in New York, Washington, D.C., Boston, Chicago, also in London, and here close to Geneva. I would call them "Lessons Inspired by C.G. Jung," and link them together through my reading of *The Red Book* and my long appreciation of *Memories, Dreams, Reflections.*

In composing *The Red Book,* Jung wrote, "I always knew that these experiences contained something precious." *(The Red Book,* p.360) It is this something precious that I wish to share in *Writing Toward Wholeness*. It is Jung's trust in the self, in who we are and who we can become.

The lessons follow Jung's own journey toward wholeness. First, there is his break with Freud in 1913 and his conscious decision to confront the unconscious. Lesson One introduces *The Red Book* and the practice of journaling to nourish the soul. Lesson Two opens the mind to active imagination through imagery, dialogues, and drawing. Lesson Three invites readers to listen to their dreams and write from them. Lesson Four illustrates the role of metaphor as a bridge between the visible world and the invisible. Lesson Five

13

explores the allure of beauty and Jung's aesthetic shaping of his visions.

As the book progresses, Lesson Six treats the study of alchemy, a subject that fascinated Jung, making him put aside his work on *The Red Book*. This led to the study of Eastern philosophies, a topic I turn to in Lesson Seven, Learning Zen. And Lesson Eight concludes the journey, bringing our experience, our language, and our sensibilities together as we write toward wholeness and approach the Self.

It is through writing that I continue to elaborate these themes, sharing them both in workshops and lectures, each time learning how to more effectively convey Jung's teaching and experience. How to do this as a writer and as someone who has experienced them through analysis, through lectures and reading, through reflection and writing. And how to en-courage—to inform and inspire—others to embark on their own journey. At every step, *Writing Toward Wholeness* reinforces the lessons Jung learned and shared with millions of people. In my first book. *Looking for Gold, A Year in Jungian Analysis,* I write about how Jung opened the door to my own journey, and now 20 years later he has led me to invite others to make their journey.

I turn to the dream Jung had as a young adult, when he found himself in a dark forest. "It was night in some unknown place and I was making slow headway against a mighty wind. Dense fog was flying everywhere. I had my hands cupped around a tiny light which threatened to go out at any moment. Everything depended on my keeping this little light alive." (*Memories, Dreams, Reflections*, 107)

This same little light is in each of us. In sharing these lessons, I wish to encourage the reader to nourish this light and take it into the world. It is in times of darkness that the light shines most brightly.

14

Chapter One

Keeping Your Own Red Books: Writing to the Soul

"I should advise you to put it all down as beautifully as you can, in some beautifully bound book…. Then you can go to the book & turn over the pages & for you it will be your church—your cathedral—the silent places of your spirit where you will find renewal…for in that book is your soul."

C.G. Jung

In our journey toward wholeness—the essential oneness of creation—each chapter presents a different path. In this first chapter we listen to C.G. Jung's words to Christiana Morgan in 1926. They are his words to us today. He urges us to direct our attention inward and to describe what we discover deep within ourselves. To put in writing the images that come to us, images from our memories, dreams, reflections. Images from the collective unconscious, that vast treasure chest of myths, folk tales, legends, artwork, shared among all cultures over the centuries. Jung is advising us to address ourselves to the imaginative possibilities of our being and write it all down in our own red books. This is the first step in the journey toward wholeness.

In this chapter I will give a short introduction to *The Red Book* and to Jung's first writings to the soul. We will look at how the soul has been viewed from earliest times until today. How did Jung see the soul? How do we see the soul?

And then how do we address the soul? We will consider how others have done, with excerpts from Etty Hillesum and Thomas Merton. To conclude, it will be our turn to write to the soul in our own red books.

1. Introduction to *The Red Book* and Jung's First Writings to the Soul

When Jung parted ways with Freud in 1913, alone and adrift, he let himself descend into the unknown, into the realm of the imagination. In *Memories, Dreams Reflections*, he writes,

> *It was during Advent of the year 1913—12th December, to be exact—that I resolved upon the decisive step. I was sitting at my desk once more thinking over my fears. Then I let myself drop. Suddenly it was as though the ground literally gave way beneath my feet, and I plunged down into dark depths. (MDR, 203)*

Stunned by visions, he called out to his soul, "My soul, where are you? Do you hear me?" An image appeared, a young maiden. Jung questioned her, listened to her, reached out to hold her hand. He described the image in his journal, recorded the encounter, and commented upon it.

More images appeared, images from centuries past of known and unknown figures—Siegfried, Elijah, Salome, Izdubar, the Red Knight, a librarian, Philemon and still others—along with images from nature of serpents and birds. He observed each one, addressed each one, then embarked on new adventures. And he continued to write it all down, knowing that otherwise the conscious mind would blot out the spontaneous fantasy. Indeed, "a running commentary is

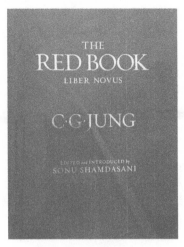

The Red Book, CG Jung
Edited and Introduced by Sonu Shamdasani

absolutely necessary…only in this painful way is it possible to gain a positive insight into the complex nature of one's own personality." (*Mysterium Coniunctionis*, par. 706).

For two years Jung continued upon this extraordinary journey that he later called Confrontation with the Unconscious. During this time, an incessant stream of visions flooded upon him, and he worked to elaborate this visionary voyage in his journals, his Black Books. Gradually, he felt the need to give these revelations a more formal elaboration. With astonishing artistic craft—antique calligraphy, illuminated borders, stunning paintings—he transcribed the visions, followed by commentaries, into a massive red leather-bound volume, the mysterious *Red Book*, titling it *Liber Novus*, the *Book of the New*.

One of the first visions that Jung embraced is the summoning of his soul. After his tense break with Freud, he realized he had lost his way. So preoccupied with his

17

professional success as a brilliant psychoanalyst, Professor at the University of Zurich, President of the International Association of Psychoanalysis, he had all but forgotten that he once had a soul. Here is his first dialogue or monologue, from the heading "Refinding the Soul" followed by a few lines from the commentary, where Jung wrestles with the image to discover its meaning.

> From the vision:
> *My soul, where are you? Do you hear me? I speak. I call you—are you there? I have returned. I am here again. I have shaken the dust of all the lands from my feet, and I have come to you. After long years of wandering, [1902-13, footnote 48, Black Book 2] I have come to you again.... What words should I use to tell you on what twisted paths a good star has guided me to you? Give me your hand, my almost forgotten soul. How warm the joy at seeing you again.... My soul, my journey should continue with you. I will wander with you and ascend to my solitude."(The Red Book, 232)*

> From the commentary:
> *The spirit of the depths forced me to say this and at the same time to undergo it against myself, since I had not expected it then.... I still labored misguidedly under the spirit of this time, and thought differently about the human soul.... I had judged her and turned her into a scientific object.... Therefore the spirit of the depths forced me to speak to my soul, to call upon her as a living being. I had to become aware that I had lost my soul. (idem, 232)*

Jung is calling out to his soul. For many years, he had listened to the exterior calling of the spirit of this time, the adulation of the intellect, of scholarship, of fame. He had achieved honor, power, wealth, knowledge, and, in his own words, every human happiness. But then, his desire for all these trappings vanished. He wanted now to shake off the dust of his worldly pursuits and heed the interior calling of the spirit of the depths. He struggled to listen to his newly found soul. Without her presence in his interior, he feared the horror of emptiness would overcome him.

All this he writes down in his journals, using the exercise of writing to unlock his imagination and deepen his reflection. He will take his time. We can picture him, sitting at his desk in his office, closing his eyes, seeing a vision of his soul, finding the words to address her, then writing down the experience. His journal entries become letters to his lost soul. "Give me your hand, my almost forgotten soul." Not wanting to let her disappear. Holding tight to her hand.

After calling out to his soul, "Where are you?" Jung asks his soul, "Who are you?" He is ignorant of its mystery. His erring through events, humanity, and the world has lasted too long. Which beyond sheltered his soul all this time? Here is the following journal entry, from the heading, "Soul and God."

From the vision:
Who are you, child? My dreams have repre-
sented you as a child, and as a maiden. I am
ignorant of your mystery. Forgive me if I speak
as in a dream, like a drunkard—are you God?
Is God a child, a maiden? Forgive me if I babble.
No one else hears me.

How strange it sounds to me to call you a
child, you who still hold the all-without-end in

19

your hand. I went on the way of the day, and you went invisibly with me, putting the pieces together meaningfully, and letting me see the whole in each part. (idem, 233)

From the commentary:
Like a tired wanderer who had sought nothing in the world apart from her, shall I come closer to my soul. I shall learn that my soul finally lies behind everything, and if I cross the world, I am ultimately doing this to find my soul....

The spirit of this time allowed me to believe in my reason. He let me see myself in the image of a leader with ripe thoughts. But the spirit of the depths teaches me that I am a servant, in fact the servant of a child. This dictum was repugnant to me and I hated it. But I had to recognize and accept that my soul is a child, and that my God in my soul is a child. (idem, 234))

The spirit of this time had misled him. He had listened only to public acclaim. Now the spirit of the depths is teaching Jung to listen to his soul. On the following night, he again wrote down all that he could remember, staying true to its wording. Disturbed by what was happening, he saw only mist and darkness. He knows not where his soul is leading him. Must he learn to follow without knowing?

Is that your meaning, my soul? I limp after you on crutches of understanding. I am a man and you stride like a God. What torture!... Hear my doubts, otherwise I cannot follow, since your meaning is a supreme meaning, and your steps are the steps of a God. (idem, 235)

Jung's writing is so visual here. We imagine him limping on crutches as he tries to follow the soul. "I am a man and you stride like a God." By letting himself address so directly the soul in writing, Jung is learning to advance without knowing in what direction.

These are some of Jung's early writings to the soul. He will continue to hold her hand, to listen to her, to follow her into the depths of his unconscious, all the while watching her grow into an independent, full-bodied adult. And he will write it all down in his journal, regarding his entries as letters to the soul.

As we read and listen to Jung's writings to the soul, we hear him urging us to do likewise. To call out to the soul, take her hand, and let her lead us. And to write it down in our own red books.

2. How Do We See the Soul?

To write to the soul, we need first to ask ourselves how we see the soul. How would we describe her? In most traditions, the soul is the spiritual essence of a person. In more contemporary language, the soul is the animating principle of the creation.

The modern word "soul" is derived from the Old English word, *sáwol*, first attested in the eighth-century poem "Beowulf." It was most likely an adaptation by early missionaries of the concept of spirit, translated from the Greek word *psyche*, meaning breath, hence life force. But meaning also soul as personified in the form of a beautiful maiden, Psyche, loved by Eros. And still another meaning in ancient Greek is butterfly, a beautiful image for the soul.

Further back in history, in ancient Egypt, the soul was a substance made up of five parts. The one most familiar to us is the Ba, the aspect of the person believed to continue to live after the body died. The Ba transformed itself into a bird with a human head leaving the mummy before burial and joining the Ka, the vital essence in the afterlife.

In ancient Greece, Plato defined the soul as the spiritual force or essence of a person, to be reborn after death in subsequent bodies. There is the surprising description of the soul growing wings in the dialogue "Phaedrus" (par. 251). Socrates is speaking of the effect of beauty on the soul. Where in seeing beauty, he imagines the soul growing wings, moistening, warming, and swelling from the root upward. Can we follow him in our imagination? Our goose bumps may be vestiges of when our souls were seen as having wings, when in taking care of them we grew feathers.

One century later, Aristotle followed in the path of Plato. In his work *On the Soul* (*De Anima*) Aristotle defines the soul as the form or essence of all living things: plants, lower animals, and humans. It is the possession of soul that gives life to an organism. It is only in one part of the human being—the mind or intellect—that the soul is a distinct substance. This part is immaterial, able to exist without the body, and therefore immortal.

Continuing through the centuries to Hildegard of Bingen in the 12th century, Abbess, theologian, mystic, for whom the soul is the greening life force of the body. Hildegard uses the word, *viriditas*, meaning greenness, vitality, lushness. Her visions picture the cosmos as a mandala, with the outer spheres representing the heavens, the inner spheres moving through sky, winds, rain to earth and to humankind. The soul is omnipresent. In her book *Scivias*,

Hildegard writes, "The Soul is not in the body, the body is in the Soul." An extraordinary insight 10 centuries ago.

Another spiritual giant of the late Middle Ages, Meister Eckhart, taught that the soul speaks in images rather than words. "When the soul wishes to experience something, she throws out an image of the experience before her and enters into her own image." Here again, this insight is remarkable. We imagine the soul throwing out an image and then entering it. And we understand in this way that she becomes one with it. We note also that Meister Eckhart identifies the soul as feminine.

Following Eckhart, theologians and mystics alike continued in their search for an understanding of the soul. Then from the 17th century onward, with the Age of Reason, whatever could not be seen with the eyes or touched with the hands was held in doubt. Only material things had substance. The physical reality of the creation was all that existed. Scientific research would give us the answers. Science would solve the riddle of our existence. In the modern mind, there is little room for the soul. Little room for the invisible, for the supernatural.

Today, modern psychologists find themselves in the middle, committed to both the material principle and the spiritual principle of reality. From 1913 onward, in his journals, Jung sought to engage with the spiritual. As he was laboring to follow his soul, he realized he was discovering his own self. "Thus your soul is your own self in the spiritual world." (*The Red Book*, p. 288) The abode of the soul is in the spiritual world, in the nonspatial universe with its untold abundance of images accumulated over millions of years. Hence, the activity of the soul is the ceaseless flow of images that moves through dreams, daydreams, fantasy, and myth. And we are back to Meister Eckhart. The soul speaks in images. As Jung moves through the flow of his images, he is journeying toward wholeness.

To conclude this rapid overview of how soul has been viewed through the centuries, I cite Jung's disciple James Hillman. In his book *The Soul's Code*, Hillman chooses the image of the acorn to represent one's soul as the potential for one's unique possibilities. Just as the oak's destiny is contained in the acorn, so our destiny is contained in our soul. Hillman gives us the lesson that true growth involves growing down into the invisible world rather than growing up into the physical world. Instead of wanting our children to grow up, we want them to grow down.

A writing suggestion:

How do you see the soul? How would you describe the soul? Perhaps close your eyes. What image comes to you? A butterfly, a maiden, an acorn? Take a moment to write a few lines.

3. How Do We Write to the Soul?

We remember that Jung advised Christina Morgan to write it all down, to write down her journey in her journal. So he advises us to do the same, to write down our journey in our journals. How do we do this? Let's look at the word "journal." We see the same root of the word, *jour* (meaning day), in both words journaling and journey. A journal is a journey, a journey to a deeper understanding of ourselves. Journaling is a spiritual practice. With our words we give life to what we see, what we touch, what we hear. We bridge the visible world and the invisible world. We find the butterfly that speaks to us of the soul.

Imagine for a moment that you are on a beach looking at the multitude of shells scattered over the sand. They are lovely, but they remain distant and indistinct. If, however, you pick up one shell and hold it in your hand, it becomes close. You see that it is unique. It is there, white and smooth. Yet one edge is jagged. It has suffered but it is still beautiful. You touch its mystery. And in writing about the shell, you discover your own smoothness, your own jagged edges. You bring the two worlds together, the visible: your shell, and the invisible: your own self.

Without a written account, it is all too easy to forget or disbelieve a memory. You forget about the flash of understanding you had when you picked up the one white shell and held it in your hand. You overlook the surprise you felt when you came upon the very same person you were recently thinking about. These synchronistic happenings point to patterns in the underlying oneness of creation. We understand synchronicity to refer to meaningful coincidences. Without paying attention to them, they retreat into forgetfulness. To journal is to slow down, to look for meaning in our experiences, and to find hints of wholeness.

I wrote in *One Year to a Writing Life* that my journals are gleanings—what I have gleaned from a walk in the Swiss vineyards, from looking at the sunrise over the Alps. I do not necessarily write every day, but I always keep my journal close at hand, one that fits into my purse, and from time to time I write down what I have gathered along the way. I write about a dream, a few words from conversation with one of my children, the morning sunlight on the surface of the lake, a quote from a book. A reflection that deepens as I write it down. Each journal entry is a step toward self-discovery, ultimately toward wholeness.

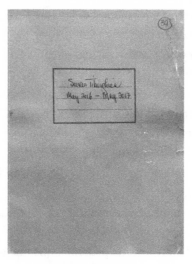

My Journal

Because my journal is always in my purse, ready to be pulled out and written in, it is a bit battered. Here is my most recent one. The edges are worn, reinforced with Scotch tape. Each journal covers between one year and two. This last one covers one year. It is not the beautiful red book, but still I find footprints of my soul on its pages.

How to start? What to write about? I turn to Rainer Maria Rilke's advice to the young man who wrote to ask how to become a poet. Rilke responded, "There is only one single way. Go into yourself." Rilke advises his young correspondent to save himself from general themes and to write about the images from his dreams, his memories, and his surroundings. "You must give birth to your images. They are the future waiting to be born." (*Letters to a Young Poet, 18-19*)

This is what Jung did in *The Red Book,* and also much later in life when he wrote his autobiography, *Memories, Dreams, Reflections.* He gave birth to his images. His friend and assistant, Aniela Jaffé, noted in her introduction to

Memories, Dreams, Reflections that "only the spiritual essence of his life's experience remained in his memory and this alone seemed to him worth the effort of telling." In his old age, only the memories which touched his soul were worth sharing.

Hence he opens his autobiography with this early memory.

> *One memory comes up which is perhaps the earliest of my life, and is indeed only a rather hazy impression. I am lying in a pram, in the shadow of a tree. It is a fine, warm summer day, the sky blue, and golden sunlight darting through green leaves. The hood of the pram has been left up. I have just awakened to the glorious beauty of the day and have a sense of indescribable well-being. (MDR, 21)*

And he ends his autobiography with this late thought.

> *There is so much that fills me: plants, animals, clouds, day and night, and the eternal in man. The more uncertain I have felt about myself, the more there has grown up in me a feeling of kinship with all things. (idem, 392)*

Jung has come full circle. He remembers from an early dream a sense of indescribable well-being that returns to him very late in life as a feeling of kinship with all things, a feeling of wholeness.

Etty Hillesum's Journals

To illustrate the depth of what can be discovered through journaling, I turn to Etty Hillesum, and her journal, *An Interrupted Life and Letters from Westerbork,* which she wrote during the last two and a half years of her life in Amsterdam and then in the transit camp for Jews at Westerbork. At the age of 29, she was deported in one of the weekly freight trains to the camps in Germany where she met her death at Auschwitz on November 30, 1943. She started her journal on March 9, 1941: "Here goes, then. This is a painful and well-nigh insuperable step for me: yielding up so much that has been suppressed to a blank sheet of lined paper." (*An Interrupted Life, 3*)

She will continue, putting down on paper what she experiences as she slowly unearths a reservoir of strength and trust that permits her to confront the unspeakable of what she is living. Days pass and the darkness grows. Here is a journal entry written a year later:

> *...the branches of the tree outside my window have been lopped off. The night before, the stars still hung like glistening fruit in the heavy branches, and now they climbed, unsure of themselves, up the bare, ravaged trunk. Oh yes, the stars: for a few nights, some of them lost, deserted, grazed over the wide forsaken plains.*
>
> *For a moment, when the branches were being cut, I became sentimental. And for that moment I was deeply sad. Then I suddenly knew: I should love the new landscape too, love it in my own way. Now the two trees rise up like imposing ascetics, thrusting into the bright sky like two daggers. (idem, 94)*

Hillesum is chronicling her day-by-day discovery of her soul. It is an astonishing account of a journey toward wholeness. With each new journal entry, her reflection deepens until she is able to transform her sadness in seeing the branches lopped off into the perception of a new landscape which she will love in her own way.

Here is another entry, another year later, from Westerbork, the transit camp from where the Jews were deported to the extermination centers in Germany. In this journal entry, Etty is addressing herself to God. The entry is contained in a letter she wrote to her friend Tide just three months before her death.

> *Darling Tide,   Westerbork, 18 August [1943]*
> *This afternoon I was resting on my bunk and suddenly I just had to write these few words in my diary, and I now send them to you:*
> *"You have made me so rich, oh God, please let me share out Your beauty with open hands. My life has become on uninterrupted dialogue with You, oh God, one great dialogue. Sometimes when I stand in some corner of the camp, my feet planted on Your earth, my eyes raised toward Your heaven, tears sometimes run down my face, tears of deep emotion and gratitude...."*
> *There are many miracles in a human life. My own is one long sequence of inner miracles, and it's good to be able to say so again to somebody.... Keep writing, please, and fare you well, my dear.*
> *Etty (idem, 332-33)*

Her last diary was lost, turned to ashes most likely at Auschwitz, but how fortunate that her friend saved her letter so that we can live in awe of the journey she made in under three years from when she started as "a miserable, frightened creature" to a celebrant of hope, a celebrant of life. She has yielded up her experiences, her reflections, her fears, her hopes, her very self, through writing.

Thomas Merton's Journals

Let us look at another contemporary of Jung, this time the Trappist monk Thomas Merton. Most people of my generation are aware of this 20th century spiritual icon, whose best-selling autobiography, *The Seven Story Mountain*, tells the story of his search for his soul, which took him from the fascination of New York City to the solitude of the Monastery of Gethsemane in the middle of Kentucky in 1941. His search took him finally to Asia, to Bangkok where he met his accidental death, electrocuted in 1968 at the age of 53. Merton continues to be a beacon of light in our darkened world. His 70-some books and collections of journals relate the many different steps on his journey toward wholeness.

Merton went as far as he could to transcend the noise, confusion and materialism of our contemporary world. The last three years of his life he lived in a hermitage in the woods bordering the monastery. This solitude brought him ever closer to the world around him, to the burning issues of racism, of civil rights, of nuclear armaments, of the war in Vietnam. His was a voice in the wilderness that was recognized recently by Pope Francis when he visited Philadelphia in September 2015 as one of the two 20th-century American Catholics to be acclaimed today. The other voice was that of Dorothy Day, a friend of Merton's and a co-worker for social justice.

Merton, in searching for his soul, was searching for himself. As he wrote in *Love and Living,* he saw the soul "not simply as the Aristotelian essential form, but the mature personal identity, the creative fruit of an authentic and lucid search, the 'self' that is found after other partial and exterior selves have been discarded as masks." (*Love and Learning,* 4) There is here a striking similarity to Jung's concept of individuation, of discarding our masks, of discovering our true self. Merton continues, "It means discovering in the ground of one's being a 'self' which is ultimate and indestructible." (idem, 5) Merton's search for the soul can be placed in parallel to Jung's search. Merton's hand-written journals find their companion in Jung's journals in his Black Books. Likewise his seven volumes of journals find their companion in *The Red Book.*

Merton kept journals for most of his adult life. He journaled to keep track of where he was in his spiritual journey through life. I had the good fortune to see his journals at the Thomas Merton Center at Bellarmine College in Louisville, Kentucky. It was John Montaldo, author, editor, and former director of the Thomas Merton Center, who showed them to me. They are kept at a cold temperature to protect the paper and the script. The cover of the journal that I examined was black. Merton wrote by hand, in beautiful script, journal entry after journal entry, page after page of blank legal paper. I saw no corrections, no deletions. Merton asked that they not be published until 25 years after his death. They are now published in seven volumes dating from 1939 to 1968, offering a candid and complete look at the transformations in his life. Brother Patrick Hart, editor of several of the series, notes that perhaps Merton's best writing can be found in the journals, for it is here where he was expressing what was deepest in his heart with no thought of censorship.

Let us look at a few of the entries, starting with short excerpts from Volume Five, 1963-1965, titled *Dancing in the Water of Life.*

> *December 9, 1964 Last night [I] went to bed late at the hermitage. All quiet. No lights. Cold. Lay in bed realizing that what I was, was happy....*

*And this morning coming down, seeing the
multitude of stars above the bare branches of the
wood, I was suddenly hit with the whole package
of meaning of everything: that the immense
mercy of God was upon me. (Dancing in the
Water of Life, 177)*

Merton is monitoring his life journey. He is experiencing
for the first time solitude in his hermitage, situated in the
woods in the outskirts of the monastery. Each entry is a letter
to the soul, to express his gratefulness and his sense of well-
being.

*May 23, 1965 One lovely dawn after another.
Such peace! Meditation with fireflies, mist in
the valley, last quarter of the moon, distant
owls—gradual inner awakening and centering
in peace and harmony of love and gratitude....
It [contemplation] implies an awareness and
acceptance of one's place in the whole.*
*May 25, 1965 Whole day at the hermitage. I
have come to see that only these days in solitude
are really full and "whole" for me. (idem, p. 250)*

Merton is approaching wholeness. His journals give us
not only a record of his life but invite us into his life, into his
thoughts and fears, his beliefs and doubts. Here is an excerpt
from *A Vow of Conversation*, Journals 1964-1965. Merton had
turned 50 and moved into the hermitage.

*September 6, 1965 Last evening, when the moon
was rising, I saw the warm burning soft red of a
doe in the field. Presently a stag came out of the
woods and then I saw a second doe and then a*

*second stag. I watched their beautiful running,
their grazing....*

*When you look at them directly and in move-
ment, you see what the primitive cave painters
saw.... It is most awe-inspiring. The 'montu' or
'spirit' is shown in the running of the deer. The
'deerness' that sums up everything and is sacred
and marvelous. (A Vow of Conversation, 207-208)*

Merton sees in the running of the deer, in the "deerness," an expression of something hidden that sums up
everything. He has seen something profound. The face of that
which is both in the deer and in himself. Merton has seen an
expression of the soul. To write about this seeing is part of
Merton's journey to wholeness.

We have seen here the paths of three spiritual giants,
CG Jung, Etty Hillesum, and Thomas Merton. How can we
follow in their footsteps? I give a more commonplace
example in turning here to my own journals, my gleanings of
what I see, hear, feel during the day. I journal to find my way
to a more conscious life, to keep track of my own journey
toward wholeness. Here is a short entry that I wrote a few
years back after my short daily walk. It was winter. The cold
was deep. The light coating of snow had frozen.

Bellevue, January 8, 2013
*On my short afternoon walk, I followed the
snow-covered foot path bordered by dark
hedges. The sky was gray and heavy. I was trying
to clear away the worries about our children and
grandchildren—the ones looking for work, the
ones not getting along, the one with cancer.
Darkness weighed on my shoulders.*

White Forsythia in Winter

There, right before me, the bush that had shriveled in the heat of summer was bursting into thousands of small white blossoms. An eruption of snow white flowers. How could such skeletal branches bring forth so much life-giving splendor? How could I not trust the same tenacity in my children and grandchildren?

I took time to first write down the experience, to describe the image and then the flash of insight that lightened the darkness. I felt gratefulness flowing though my words. A shriveled bush bursting into bloom in the middle of winter. I looked up the name of such a bush on internet. The closest I could come was "white forsythia," a shrub that blossoms with white, star-shaped flowers from pink buds in early spring before the true forsythia. I liked the early spring. New growth was coming even in January.

A few days later, I went back to the icy, snow-covered path and took a photo of my white winter forsythia bush. Again the beauty of the pink buds bursting into white flowers there in the snow set my heart alight.

Still today, I can return to my journal entry and renew my trust in small miracles. More deeply my trust in nature. What better gift from journaling? I imagine that Jung returned often to his journal entries, and to the paintings that he so exquisitely did to illustrate his encounters, paintings that he included in *The Red Book*. Each time feeling anew the emotion and deepening his understanding of the experience he was putting into words. Here in his journals was "the *prima materia* for a lifetime's work." Here were the traces of the soul leading him to wholeness.

A writing suggestion:

Imagine sharing a memory with the soul. Let the memory come to you, a recent one, or perhaps one from childhood. Write it as a journal entry, starting with the date and place. Let your words take you into this "silent place of the spirit."

In conclusion, we listen anew to Jung's summons to Christina Morgan to write it all down in a beautiful red book. Jung is speaking to all of us, urging us to write it all down. To write down our experiences, our feelings and thoughts, as we live our days. To follow the images that come to us, letting them lead us into the invisible world where the soul will take us by the hand on our journey to wholeness.

Chapter Two

Pursuing Images: Active Imagination

"The years when I was pursuing my inner images were the most important time of my life—in them everything essential was decided. It was the *prima materia* for a lifetime's work."
C.G. Jung

As we follow Jung's path in *The Red Book*, we will look in this chapter at how he pursued the images in his visions. How he gave them life, moving from a vision to a face-to-face encounter. We will see how he confronts his soul who speaks back to him. How he listens and learns. We will acquaint ourselves with his experience of active imagination. Of actively imagining a figure, visualizing it, listening to it, entering into dramatic experience with it, and then writing it down in order to safeguard its happening and not belittle the experience with our minds. As Jung journeyed to wholeness, active imagination was his walking stick.

The chapter will have four parts. First, Jung's experience with active imagination. How is it practiced? A second section will treat dialoguing with the images and figures of our imagination, one form of active imagination. A third section will treat drawing and painting the images, another form of active imagination, with reference to mandalas. In each section, examples from *The Red Book* will be included. And lastly, we will look at how two contemporary authors, Orhan Pamuk and Terry Tempest Williams, pursued their images.

They will serve as examples of how we can do likewise as we let our images map our life journey.

1. Jung's Experience with Active Imagination

Overcome by the twice-repeated vision of a monstrous flood covering all the land between the North Sea and the Alps, Jung was at a loss to understand. He heard an inner voice: "Look at it well; it is wholly real and it will be so." To proceed, Jung knew he had to let himself 'plummet down' into the fantasies that were stirring underground. It was December 12, 1913. He was sitting at his desk and decided to let himself drop. "Suddenly it was as though the ground literally gave way beneath my feet, and I plunged down into dark depths." (*MDR*, 203)

This was the beginning of *The Red Book,* the story of Jung's confrontation with the unconscious, his deliberate encounter with his inner images. We read in the first chapter how he called out to his lost soul, aroused her image, the image of a young maiden. How he questioned her and asked to hold her hand. All this he did in his imagination, summoning the image, dialoguing with it, then recording the vision in writing and commenting upon it. He pursued his visions for 16 years, all the while seeing his patients and encouraging them to do the same. As he did for Christiana Morgan in 1926: "I should advise you to put it all down as beautifully as you can, in some beautifully bound book." This was the *prima materia* for all his future work and accomplishments.

We do not have to dramatically plummet down into our dark depths as Jung did in order to summon our inner images. Yet, I can remember saying to Keller, my analyst, during one of our first sessions, that I wanted to stamp on the ground until it opened up and let me drop into its depths. I was reading *Faust* and was admittedly inflated. I wanted to challenge Mephistopheles. Keller was not impressed and asked me instead if I had a dream to share.

It is easier to remember Rilke's advice to the young man who asked Rilke how to become a poet: "There is only one single way. Go into yourself..." Look within and use to express yourself the images of your dreams, memories, and surroundings. So to summon our images, we close our eyes and look inward. We shut out the physical world around us, the noises, interruptions, distractions. And we enter the world of our imagination.

The psyche speaks to us in images: pictures, representations, likenesses. Jung saw these images as clues or tips that reveal our inner state, that point to the meaning of what we are living. The image, whether present in nature, in a memory, or in our imagination, leads us to a deeper understanding of the mystery of our life. If, when I close my eyes, I often see a maple tree, I need to ask myself why. What is it telling me? Is it speaking of my roots in America and the branches in Switzerland? How in my daily life I look continually to bring together the two cultures, the two languages? Or is it now speaking of old age, of time to let the leaves fall to the ground and return to the roots? Time to let go and look for longer moments of silence and meditation. The image of a maple tree leading me to unfold my life story.

Once we close our eyes and let the image emerge from our unconscious, how do we pursue it? Jung described the procedure he used during his confrontation with the unconscious as active imagination, taking one image at a time and giving it life. He was doing, as we remember from chapter one, what Meister Eckhart, the German theologian and mystic, six centuries earlier was teaching. "When the soul wants to experience something..." she throws out an image and steps into it. Jung's visions emerged from deep within his psyche. He stepped into them. The images became the characters and settings that he wrote into his journals—*The Black Books*—and then transcribed into *The Red Book*.

In *Mysterium Coniunctionis* (CW 14, par.706), Jung gives a careful description of active imagination. He completed this last major work in his 81ˢᵗ year. The well-known analyst Edward Edinger wrote that this work was really the summa of Jungian psychology. Jung believed that "we must turn back to those periods in human history when symbol formation still went on unimpeded." When one could fantasize at liberty. He was referring to medieval natural philosophy, to the world of alchemy which he thought stood in a close relationship to the psychology of the unconscious. I write about alchemy later in Chapter Six. Here, I return to Jung's description of active imagination as a bridge between the conscious and the unconscious. He is describing the way to work with an image. In taking direct quotes from this paragraph, I list five suggested steps to the process, ones that we can follow in our own active imaginations.

Steps to Active Imagination

—First, "choose a dream or some other fantasy-image and concentrate on it by simply catching hold of it and looking at it."

— "Then fix this image in the mind. Usually it will alter as the mere fact of contemplating it animates it."

— "A chain of fantasy ideas develops and gradually takes on a dramatic character.... At first it consists of projected figures and these images are observed like scenes in the theatre."

—"If the observer understands that his own drama is being performed on this inner stage...he will take part in the play instead of just sitting in a theatre."

—"Fix the whole procedure in writing at the time of occurrence for you then have ocular evidence that will effectively counteract tendency to self-deception."

It is essential to note that to follow the steps, we need to put ourselves in a meditative state. Our conscious minds are relaxed, letting us enter the inner world of our imagination. We quiet ourselves, we let go of our worries, thoughts, and preoccupations. Once we are in this state, we choose an image, or better, we let the image choose us. (1) We hold on to it. (2) We watch it take life. (3) We put it on the stage of our imagination and observe it. (4) We get up on the stage and take part in the play, in its story which in reality is our story. (5) And then we write down what happened.

The last step is crucial. Without it, we will downplay the experience, we will not listen to its teaching, we will continue as if it did not happen. As Jung wrote in his Commentary to *The Secret of the Golden Flower*, "The task consists solely in objectively observing a fragment of a fantasy in its development. Nothing could be simpler, and yet right here the difficulties begin.... The conscious mind raises prolific objections." (*The Secret of the Golden Flower*, 93) We don't want to believe that our fantasies have any sense or meaning. We tell ourselves, it is just our imagination. But exactly, our imagination is what is most precious to our inner life. And yet we belittle it, we think it worthless. Our conscious mind "seems bent upon blotting out the spontaneous fantasy-activity in spite of real insight.... Often a veritable cramp of consciousness exists." (ibid.) A cramp of consciousness can close the door to the unconscious.

41

It is to counteract this cramp of consciousness that Jung counsels us to write down what happened. Our active imaginations will give us teachings. The image will speak to us, will surprise us with a lesson. If we do not write it down, we will not only forget the experience, we will forget the teaching. If I did not write down my dialogue with the maple tree, I would still be holding on to all my leaves. Instead, as I return to my journal entry, I remember, and slowly I drop a few leaves, a few of the too many activities, the too many preoccupations, the too many personal concerns that leave me breathless at the end of the day.

From 1913 onward, for several years, Jung devoted himself to this inner work, to doing one active imagination after another and to writing down the experiences followed by his commentaries in *The Black Books*. The work was extremely rigorous, tiring, and disabling him often, making him wonder if he were not going mad. He claimed afterward that it was only in being able to express his intense emotions in images that saved his reason.

Then with artistry and calligraphy, he transcribed his words into *The Red Book,* adding extraordinary paintings. In 1917, he added a fresh manuscript called the *Scrutinies*. The editor, Sonu Shamdasani, in his Introduction to *The Red Book*, writes that the complete sequence of *The Red Book* would be: *Liber Primus: The Way of What is to Come, Liber Secondus: The Images of the Erring*, and *Liber Tertius: Scrutinies*.

We are extraordinarily privileged today to have access to this complete sequence, to this lived experience of Jung's exploration of the unconscious. As we open *The Red Book* and turn the pages, we dip into it as we would dip into a mysterious well for refreshment. We open a door to our own exploration of the unconscious.

2. Dialoguing with Images

One form of active imagination that Jung used, and that he counseled his patients to use, is to speak to our images, to dialogue with them. Once we have fixed an image in our attention, we can ask it questions. Why did it come to us? What does it have to say to us? What are we to now do? We listen to what the image answers. We let ourselves be surprised. And we write down the dialogue as we would if we were writing a story. Indeed we are writing a story, a real story.

Let's look at one of the active imaginations that Jung did early in his journey into the unconscious, when he continues his dialogue with his soul, who has grown from the wispy maiden into an adult woman. Jung imagines himself in a dreary desert seeking solace from the heat. He hears the spirit of this time telling him to return to his professional work and abandon the confrontation. He is fearful, even nauseated, ready to give up, until he hears the voice of the spirit of the depths: "Look into your depths, pray to your depths." Disoriented and at a loss, he reaches for the hand of his soul. This vision and dialogue come from the sections titled "The Desert and Experiences in the Desert" in *Liber Primus*. I have set up the conversation in the form of a dialogue with excerpted quotes.

> *My soul leads me into the desert, into the desert of my own self. I did not think that my soul is a desert, a barren hot desert, dusty and without drink.... How eerie is this wasteland. It seems to me that the way leads so far away from mankind.*
>   *"My soul, what am I to do here?"*
> *My soul spoke to me and said, "Wait."*

43

"I would like to sit down near you and at least feel the breath of your animating presence....You are to me like a shady tree in the wilderness. I would like to enjoy your shade."

"You are pleasure seeking. Where is your patience? Your time has not yet run its course. Have you forgotten why you went into the desert?"

"My faith is weak, my face is blind from all that shimmering blaze of the desert sun. I dare not think how unendingly long my way is, and I see nothing in front of me."

"You speak as if you have still learned nothing. Can you not wait? Should everything fall into your lap ripe and finished? You are full, yes, you teem with intentions and desires! Do you still not know that the way to truth stands open only to those without intentions?"

"You are hard, my soul, but you are right. We should grow like a tree that does not know its law. We tie ourselves up with intentions not mindful of the fact that intention is limitation."
(The Red Book, 236)

The soul has now become an adult with whom Jung may dialogue. Someone who responds, someone who reprimands. Someone who is teaching him. Teaching this person who at the age of 40 was at his zenith: married to a brilliant woman, five children, president of the International Association of Psychoanalysis, professor at the University of Zurich. His soul is telling him to be patient, to wait. Jung listens to her hard but salutary words. He needs her to take him in hand. She will accompany him on his voyage where eventually he will uncover a new understanding of his own self and a new image of the God figure. Where he will develop a new worldview in the form of a psychological cosmology.

I remember well when I first tried an active imagination. It was in the early months of my analysis, and Keller asked if I knew anything about active imagination. I said I knew of it only from my reading. He suggested I try. I should speak to the cat who was appearing often in both my night and day dreams. I thought this was far-fetched and foolish, but I wanted to try. I lay down on my bed one afternoon and summoned my cat. It was a tabby cat, who lately had been coming in the window and going under my bed. When I felt my cat was there anew, resting under my bed, I said aloud, "What do you want?" I had to ask three times before it responded. I wrote about the experience in my first book, *Looking for Gold*, the chapter "Cat at the Door." The cat said it just wanted to stay there and rest. Its advice that I, too, should rest and take catnaps is still valid today.

I continue to dialogue with the images of my dreams and imaginings. Here is an account of a recent active imagination, one with the tree that I mentioned earlier. This happened during a seminar that I was giving to a group of writers and analysts here in Switzerland. I was speaking about active imagination and asking the participants to follow Jung's suggested steps. I followed along and closed my eyes, trying to empty the screen of my mind, waiting for an image to appear. A tree with fall foliage appeared, like the one outside my kitchen window. Its rust colored leaves were falling sporadically to the ground. I spoke to it. Here is the dialogue as I wrote it in my journal.

November 6, 2015
I: Why again have you come to me?
Tree: To encourage you.

I: To encourage me to do what? To look at you,
to admire your colors?
Tree: And still more.
I: To watch the leaves fall?
Tree: And still more.
I: To let the leaves fall?
Tree: Yes, to let them fall on their own.
I: How do I do this?
Tree: You loosen your control.
I: I stop checking if all is well? Stop worrying
about family, friends, about my work.
Tree: Right. You let things be.
I: I should sit back and let the leaves fall.
Tree: You sit back physically but at the same time
you keep growing. You become lighter, freer.
I: I keep growing?
Tree: The leaves return to the roots to rise anew.
I: Life follows death?
Tree: Yes, they are a continuum.
With these last words, I see the tree lean down
to the ground, shaping itself into a circle. I feel
energy rising through me. I too want to lean
down and touch the ground.

By actively engaging the tree, by asking questions and
listening to answers, I was given a lesson concerning life and
death. At the end of the dialogue I saw the tree represented as
a circle, bending down to touch the earth. The tree became a
uniting symbol, relating the known and the unknown. The
known was what is outside my kitchen window, what I am
doing in my daily life. The unknown was both my roots and
what was ahead of me. Jung calls this process the transcendent
function, bringing together opposites, the known and the

unknown, and creating something new. I bring together the leaves and the roots, the visible and the invisible, and I create new freedom and new life.

I copy my dialogues into my journal, each time with the date. I comment on them. Step by step the dialogues lead me to new discoveries, to a deeper understanding of myself. A way of writing toward wholeness.

A writing suggestion:

Try now to do an active imagination in the form of writing a dialogue with an inner image. Close your eyes to clear your mind. Let an image emerge. Hold on to it. Ask it why it came to you. Write your question in the form of a dialogue. Let the image respond. Let yourself be surprised.

In writing this dialogue, you are fixing in writing your active imagination. Afterward, when you might disbelieve that your image spoke to you, when you might even forget the whole episode, you will have it here in your journal. You can turn to it and listen anew. Your journal is the silent place of the spirit.

3. Drawing Images

Dialoguing with an image is only one way of active imagination. There are other ways to enter into the drama that unfolds as we look at our image. We could get on the stage and act out the tree, become the tree. We could sway lightly, letting our arms rise and fall, moving our hands as the wind lifts them, and then bending down and touching the earth. We would feel the letting go. We would become ourselves a circle. Or we could draw the tree, the dark trunk, the branches that narrow as they reach towards the light, the bright foliage. If we have colored pencils, the blue sky, the reddish leaves suspended in space, the brown earth. In doing this, we give our full attention to our image. We step into it.

This is what Jung did as he recorded his visions in *The Red Book*. He painted many of them, in stunning colors, slowly, carefully, giving them life. Many of us are familiar with the brilliant full-page paintings illustrating the inner images of *Liber Secundus*. Let me mention here a less familiar one, a smaller, earlier drawing in *Liber Primus*. At the head of the first page of Gothic lettering in Latin and in German, there is a capital D, behind which is a landscape. In the upper part of the painting, Jung has painted the roofs of a city, a church steeple, the mountains, clouds, and blue, blue sky. In the lower part, he has painted a boat and an underwater world, two large fish, all sorts of sea growth. The spirit of the depths is calling Jung to descend into the unconscious, into the underworld. To leave behind the spirit of this time and the bustling city where he lives, always busy with research, lectures, colleagues, students, and patients. Two opposite worlds. Two opposing spirits.

As Jung took the time to intricately paint the two worlds where he found himself at the beginning of his journey, he freed his mind to enter into the vision. We can picture him listening to the spirit of this time, telling him to stay in the upper world where he is known and acclaimed, while the spirit of the depths is inviting him to descend into the lower world, into his unconscious.

There are very few of us who can even start to approach Jung's artistic talent, but we can draw our images simply with a pencil in our journals. As we do, we quiet the thousand thoughts rushing through our mind and we enter the world of the image. Often in my journal, after writing about something

I saw, something most often in the natural world, I will draw the image in the margin. I will slowly pencil in the different shades of gray. It is an exercise in active imagination. I enter into the image and learn a lesson.

Here is one I drew of the tree with whom I dialogued in my journal entry. It barely looks like a tree, but when I return to it, I see the roots, a few branches, with leaves ready to fall. I see that the tree is bending down to the ground, shaping itself into a circle.

Tree Bending Down

The drawing shows me the continuum, from the roots to the leaves and back to the roots. Life is a continuum. There is energy moving through it. I feel strengthened and renewed. A tree bowing down to the ground.

Another way to creatively engage your image is to draw it in a mandala. Drawing mandalas is a centering practice that leads us to wholeness. Mandala is the Sanskrit word for circle, the symbol of the cosmos in its entirety. In a later work, *The Archetypes and the Collective Unconscious*, Jung explains the importance he gave to the mandala.

> *The universality of the mandala lies in its one constant: the principle of the center, the source of all creative energy. In the center all is one. Whether it is manifested in a star, a rose or a human being, there is cosmic communion.... There is the movement of birth from the center towards a world of creative differentiation. Then there is the return movement towards the unity of the center and the potential of new life. (Collected Works, Volume 9, Part I)*

When we look at a mandala, our attention is drawn to the center, then outward. And then back to the center. We cannot keep looking at the center. When we look outward, the world is differentiated. So we are drawn to look back to the center where all is one. It is the same movement with breathing. We cannot keep breathing in; we have to breathe out. And then in again. The principle of the center. The rhythm of the creation.

The first representations of mandalas go back to Paleolithic times; they are concentric circles, sun wheels, carved into cliffs in Transvaal, South Africa, estimated to be 60,000 years old. In Tibetan Buddhism, the mandala is a circular representation of the cosmos in its connection with divine powers. Used as an object of meditation, it leads to at-oneness with the world. Following the mandala through the centuries, there is Hildegard of Bingen, the 11th century Abbess, mystic, theologian, healer, musician, who drew several of her visions in beautiful mandalas, etching them onto wax tablets. Two centuries later, the rose windows in Gothic cathedrals were created to uplift the soul and approach the divine. In Native American tradition, the sand-painting mandalas are still used today for healing. In all traditions, the mandala represents the search for wholeness.

Jung drew his first mandala in 1916, titling it "Systema munditotius, The Systems of All Worlds." It is a highly detailed depiction of the universe that came to him in a vision that I describe at length in Chapter Eight. During the following years, he drew numerous mandalas, many of which figure in *The Red Book*. By moments overwhelmed with the stream of visions flooding his imagination, he unconsciously turned to drawing mandalas to restore balance and order within himself.

Let us look at one of them, from *Liber Secundas*, that illustrates his efforts to impose some sort of order upon the chaos surrounding him. The painting accompanies the following words in the text: "I accepted the chaos, and in the following night, my soul approached me." (*The Red Book,* 298) He drew this beautiful mandala, with the star of light in the center radiating outward beyond two inner circles, to the four directions of the cross, north south, east, west. And the whole protected by the two outer circles. Jung is painting here an image of harmony presiding over chaos.

My Soul Approached Me, C.G. Jung
Image 107, The Red Book

Jung called his mandalas "cryptograms," showing his state of mind when he drew the mandala. In drawing and painting mandalas, Jung came to understand that all the paths he had been following were leading back to the midpoint, to the center. All the steps we take, all our dreams, our memories, our reflections lead us to the center of our being.

Jung was gifted in so many astonishing ways. His paintings inspire awe. We are humbled to even think we can follow his example. However, we can try. When I journal, often I am led to create a mandala, to draw the image I am writing about—an image from my surroundings, from a dream or a memory, or from my imagination—and place it in a mandala. My journals contain many small mandalas, drawn slowly with a pencil. I draw a circle maybe three or four centimeters in circumference. Then a smaller circle in the middle. I draw my image most often in the center, but sometimes I let it circle the center. And I give my mandalas titles. In naming them this way, I honor them. I give them life.

There follows one I drew during a workshop at the Jung Society in Washington, D.C. It was in the spring, and I was in awe in front of the blossoming dogwoods. We do not have many dogwood trees in Switzerland. In April, they are glorious on the East Coast. The dogwood blossom that I drew was white. As I drew the four petals, with one petal longer than the other three, I remembered the legend that Christ was crucified on a dogwood tree. The petals form a cross, and they are tipped with dark red, representing the blood that was shed, the seeds in the center represent the crown of thorns. I saw the light radiating out from the very dark center, in the four directions of the cross, north south, east, west. As I closed my eyes, I could see the four rays of light turning.

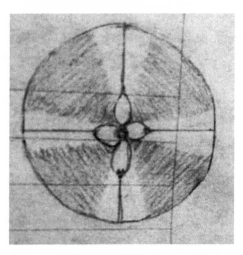

Dogwood Blossom

When I look back at the pages of my journals, often it is the drawing, the mandala, that first calls my attention. I remember the experience. I feel again the emotion that was mine when I was drawing it. Jung writes, "By being charged with emotion, the image gains numinosity (or psychic energy); it becomes dynamic." (*Man and His Symbols*, 87) My mandalas are alive. They show me where I am on my life's journey toward wholeness. Soul maps.

Drawing often is a very effective way of active imagination. It takes us sometimes out of our safety zones. It quiets our rational mind. In so doing, our imagination has a free hand. Before moving on and reading about two contemporary authors and how they pursue their images, let's return to our image and draw it in a mandala.

A drawing suggestion:

Take a piece of paper and pencil and draw a circle. In the center draw another circle, the size that you wish. Now place your image where you wish and fill in the mandala. You are drawing toward wholeness.

4. Reading Two Contemporary Authors

Orhan Pamuk

We will look now at how two contemporary writers pursue their images. First, Orhan Pamuk. If we consider his prizewinning novel, *Snow,* from the title and the very first page, Pamuk is pursuing the image of snow. The narrator Ka, a journalist and poet, is leaving Istanbul by bus to travel across Turkey to Kars to supposedly cover a suicide epidemic, but truthfully to find a lost love and hopefully to hear again the voice of his muse. Note that the Turkish word for snow is kar. Ka to Kars to kar.

Already on the first page, as Ka sets out from Istanbul by bus for Kars, he is caught in a snowstorm. The flakes were falling heavier and heavier, isolating Ka even in the bus.

> *The silence of snow, thought the man sitting just behind the bus-driver.... If he hadn't been so tired, if he'd paid more attention to the snowflakes swirling out of the sky like feathers, he might have realized that he was travelling straight into a blizzard. (Snow, 3)*

Soon after Ka's arrival in Kars, the growing blizzard isolates the city from the outside world. Ka loses all sense of himself in the falling snow. He no longer knows what he is doing in the world. A man lives his life and then falls apart. Like a snowflake, he, too, would fall. He pulls up memories of his childhood, the certain smell of his father after shaving, his mother making breakfast, her slippers on the cold kitchen floor.

> *As he gave his mind over to all such little things that make up a life...he saw a snowflake.*

And so it was that Ka heard the call from deep inside him, the call he heard at moments of inspiration: the sound of his muse. For the first time in four years a poem was coming to him. (idem, 88)

Ka hurried through the snow back to his hotel. He opened his green notebook and wrote down the poem as it came to him, word by word. He titled the poem "Snow."

Much later, when he thought about how he'd written this poem, he had a vision of a snowflake. This snowflake, he decided, was his life writ small. (idem, 89)

The novel continues, and the reader learns that in his notebook, Ka drew a snowflake, slowly placing the poems he would now write around the six points of its hexagon shape under the three axes: memory, logic, and imagination. A snowflake mapping out his life, a hexagonal mandala. He placed I, Ka, in the center. The drawing is included in the novel to let the reader discover and appreciate the hidden symmetries that the author is seeking to reveal.

A single snowflake, a single life. Pamuk, in pursuing the image of snow, has brought together the visible physical world of a snowflake with his own invisible spiritual world. He has bridged the two worlds.

Terry Tempest Williams

I turn to another contemporary author, Terry Tempest Williams, an ecologist and social activist and a brilliant writer. In her book, *When Women Were Birds, Fifty-four Variations on Voice*, Williams is 54, the age her mother was when she died. One week before, they were lying on her mother's bed with a mohair blanket covering them. Her mother was dying in the same way she was living, consciously.

> *"I am leaving you all my journals," she said, facing the shuttered window.... "But you must promise me that you will not look at them until after I am gone."....*
> *They were exactly where she said they would be: three shelves of beautiful clothbound books.... I opened the first journal. It was empty. I opened the second journal. It was empty. I opened the third. It too was empty...shelf after shelf after shelf, all my mother's journals were blank. (When Women Were Birds, 3-4)*

Her mother was Mormon. Williams writes that in Mormon culture women are expected to bear children and keep journals. She does not know why her mother bought journal after journal, year after year. Nor why she never wrote in one of them and then passed them on to her. The blow of the blank pages became a second death.

> *My Mother's Journals are paper tombstones.*
> *(idem, 17)*

From these first pages onward, Williams holds on to the image of the blank pages of her mother's journals. She writes on them, not with a pen, but a pencil, because she likes the idea of erasure. She realizes that her mother has been erased. From first seeing the journals as tombstones, Williams imagines them in innumerable different ways, reflecting her search to understand.

> *My Mother's Journals are my desire to know.*
> *(idem, 25)*

The book is a meditation on voice and the mystery of her mother's journals. Williams asks herself what she is gleaning in the furrows of her mother's journals. She forages for the details overlooked to find out what is there and what is not there. As she pursues the image of the white page, she is pursuing her mother's voice and her own voice.

> *Mother gave me my voice by withholding hers, both in life and in death.... I will never know what she was trying to tell me by telling me nothing. But I can imagine. (idem, 150, 154)*

Her mother could not write in her journals and remain true to herself. She did not want to hurt those she loved if her journals were read. And in the Mormon culture, women are raised to believe their journals will be read by the future.

> *My Mother's Journals are an awakening. (idem, 204)*

Williams asks herself how shall she live. She wants to feel both the beauty and the pain of the age she is living in. She wants to be guided by the songs of birds. When women were birds, there was the understanding that to sing at dawn and then at dusk is to heal the world. Birds still remember that the world is meant to be celebrated.

> *My Mother's Journals are to be celebrated. (idem, 206)*

Williams has stepped into the image. The blank pages are to be celebrated. In staying with the image of her mother's journals, Williams has passed on to us the gift that her mother gave her, the gift of love.

A writing suggestion:

Return to your image and write a journal entry about how you pursued it—the dialogue, the drawing. And what the image revealed to you. These short writings may become pages in your red book.

In conclusion, may this lesson, "Pursuing Your Images: Active Imagination," accompany you on your life journey. As Jung wrote, "The years when I was pursuing my inner images were the most important time of my life—in them everything essential was decided." The bedrock of Jung's journey to wholeness was the pursuit of his inner images. So may it be for you as you map your own life journey toward wholeness.

Chapter Three

Exploring Dreams: Listening and Writing

"The dream is a little hidden door in the innermost and most
secret recesses of the psyche, opening into that cosmic night
which was psyche, long before there was any ego consciousness
and which will remain psyche no matter how far our ego
consciousness may extend."
C.G. Jung

In this chapter we will examine how dreams are in the
service of wholeness. How they open the door to the
unconscious, bridging the physical world and the dream
world. In so doing dreams reveal the essential oneness of the
psyche and of the creation, of the soul and the body. C.G. Jung
urges us to enter the doorway of our dreams. As thoughts of
our psyche, they show us where we are in the narrative of our
life. What is our life story? This is the question Jung asks us:
"What is your myth—the myth in which you do live?"

We will review how dreams have been listened to
throughout history and then look at how Jung listened to his
Liverpool dream that he titled "Window to Eternity." How
can we follow his example? I will suggest steps to help us
explore our own dreams. We will consider excerpts from the
work of contemporary authors who have mined their dreams
to write from them. The chapter ends with the suggestion that

we mine our own dreams to find our life story and write its pages.

1. Dreams and Dream Interpretation
Throughout the Centuries

From the dawn of history, dreams have intrigued humanity. The earliest recorded dreams date back to around 3200 B.C.E. and were written first in pictures, then in cuneiform on clay tablets in Mesopotamia. Dreams were considered to be sent by the gods. Dream priests interpreted the dreams, foretelling the dreamer's future. There is the record of Gilgamesh's first dream, predicting the arrival of Enkidu, who was to become his companion. Gilgamesh was the semi-mythic King of Uruk around 2500 B.C.E. It is interesting for our study of *The Red Book* to note that Jung gave Gilgamesh the name of Izdubar, which was the name used in the first publication in English in 1872, when there was difficulty in reading cuneiform. We will read about Jung's encounter with Izdubar in Chapter Seven.

The pharaohs in Egypt were also paying attention to dreams, using them to predict both good and bad fortune. Dream temples were devoted to Serapis, the Egyptian God of dreams. At Memphis, the earliest dream temple dates back to 3000 B.C.E. There were rituals including cleansing and fasting, with prayers and chants. Professional dream interpreters resided in the temples. A clay tablet was found with the message, "I interpret dreams, having the gods' mandate to do so. Good luck. The interpreter present here is Cretan." A very early calling card for a dream analyst.

In Judaism, dreams figure prominently in the Old Testament. The Hebrews connected their dreams with their religion, believing that dreams were the voice of their one God. There is Jacob's dream (Gen. 28:12), where alone on a hill top, he sleeps with his head on a stone and sees a ladder with angels ascending and descending. Yahweh is standing over him, "And behold, I am with thee." Jacob rises early in the morning, sets the stone up as a pillar and pours oil on its top. He names the site Bethel, the house of God.

Jacob's 11th son, Joseph, shared the following dream with his brothers. "Hear this dream I have dreamed. Behold we were binding sheaves in a field and behold my sheaf rose and stood upright. And behold your sheaves gathered around it and bowed down to my sheaf." (Gen. 37:6-7) It is evident that his brothers did not appreciate Joseph's dream. And indeed they sold him into slavery. But he rose to become second in power in Egypt, and his brothers did come and bow down to him.

In the New Testament, dreams were also seen as prophetic. There are the four dreams of Joseph, Mary's fiancé and husband in the Gospel of Matthew. In the first, Joseph is told to not be afraid to take Mary as his wife since she has conceived by the Holy Spirit (Mat.1:20). Then Joseph is warned "to take the child and His mother and flee to Egypt" for Herod is searching to destroy the child (Mat. 2:13) In the third, he is told to return into the land of Israel "for those who sought the child's life are dead." (Mat. 2:19). And lastly Joseph is warned to not go to Judaea, so he leaves for Galilee and settles in Nazareth. (Mat. 2:23)

I turn to dreams in ancient China where the masters in the Taoist schools saw dreams as allegories for the human condition. There is the famous story of Chuang Tzu, 350 B.C.E., who, after dreaming about the happiness of being a butterfly, woke and no longer knew if he were a butterfly or a man. "I do not know whether I was then a man dreaming I was a butterfly or whether I am not a butterfly dreaming I am a man."

Likewise in Indian beliefs, in the Upanishads, it is written that dreams fill the gap between the inner knowing and the outer knowing. In 544 B.C.E., Buddha's mother, Queen Maya, dreamed her bed was transported by four kings to a high Himalayan peak, where four queens adorned her with jewels and brought her to a golden palace. A white elephant appeared and painlessly pierced her side with a thrust of its shining ivory tusk. She awoke to the song of a blue bird and realized she had immaculately conceived. Her dream was interpreted to signify that her child would become a universal monarch.

In ancient Greece, as in Egypt, people turned to dreams for solutions for healing and foretelling the future. Healing temples were dedicated to the Greek God of Medicine, Asclepius, born of a divine father Apollo and mortal mother Coronis and raised by Chiron the Centaur. Dream incubation and healing were practiced, with patients sleeping overnight and reporting their dreams to priests the following day. The most famous temple was built in the fifth century B.C.E. at Epidaurus. In the middle of the temple, there was a sacred well with nonvenomous snakes used in healing rituals. Each night, when the lamps were extinguished, the dreamers listened to these words: "Sleep now, dream now, dream the dream of the healing God, the God who will come in the night. Sleep now, dream now." Words that have echoed throughout the centuries and that we may still recite today.

Moving forward, dreams continued to be regarded as a source of healing and instruction. There was Synesius, a Greek bishop born in Libya, in the fifth century C.E. He is the author of the book *On Dreams*, which remains perhaps the most thorough study of dreams until the modern day work of Freud and Jung. To help a person discover the relation between waking events and dream imagery, Synesius was the first to encourage people to keep dream journals.

This brings us to Islam and 620 C.E., when Muhammad received his divine mission in a dream. In his famous *Night Journey*, (*Quran*, surah 17) he traveled on a white mare first to Jerusalem, then to Heaven. Guided by the angel Gabriel he entered the House of Adoration, and together they approached the throne of Allah. Allah gave Muhammad instructions to take back to the faithful regarding prayer. They were to pray five times daily. Much of the Quran was revealed to Muhammad in dreams over several subsequent years. Each morning, he would share his dreams with his disciples and ask about theirs.

In the Catholic Church during the Middle Ages, there is Francis of Assisi, whose life was turned around by a dream. Francis, born into a noble family in the 13th century, aspired to become a knight and find glory on the battlefield. On his way to Rome to join the papal armies, he stopped at Spoleto for the night. In his sleep, God spoke to him. "Who can do more for you, the lord or the servant?" Francis responded, "The lord, of course." And God answered, "Then why do you leave the lord for the servant?" God instructed him to return home, and there it would be revealed to him what he must do. Because of his dream, Francis became a knight for Christ.

Then during the last centuries of the Medieval Period, demons and devils became an obsessive concern for the Catholic Church and its adherents. Aquinas warned against demons in dreams. And Luther went so far as to pray to God to not remember his dreams. Dreams were associated with Satanism and witchcraft. Many Christians believed that humans could make pacts with the devil and sell their souls for riches. The German schoolmaster named Faust, living in the 1500s, made such a pact.

We arrive at the Age of Reason in the 17th century, with philosophers Locke and Descartes. Descartes set up his Argument about Dreaming to prove that the senses were not to be trusted. Descartes and his followers argued that true knowledge comes only through the strict application of reason. Moving into the Age of Enlightenment in the 18th century, scientific rigor ruled the day. Whatever could not be physically proven was distrusted. The distrust continued into the 19th century, with the belief that dreams were without any real meaning or significance.

It was Freud (1856-1939) who, with his *Interpretation of Dreams,* published in 1900, revived the importance of dreams after so many centuries of neglect. He believed that dreams come from our unconscious, reflecting our deepest wishes and anxieties, often related to early childhood experiences. He described dreams as "the royal road to the unconscious" and is referred to as the father of psycho-analysis, the study of the unconscious level of the psyche.

C.G. Jung (1875-1961), his colleague and then his rival, expanded Freud's theory of the unconscious, seeing it not only as the personal unconscious but also, at a deeper level, as the collective unconscious, our common heritage of myths, folklore, and dream images. He defined the dream as "a little hidden door in the innermost recesses of the psyche opening into the cosmic night of the unconscious." From these innermost recesses, dreams present revelations concerning both the life experience of the dreamer and the mystery of human existence.

Both of these men brought to the world of psychology the necessary scientific status to establish recognition of the existence of the unconscious, the importance of dreams, and the value of psychoanalysis. In our century, dreams and dreaming are acknowledged as messengers of the unconscious mind. Robert Johnson, in the introduction to his book *We,* writes that by learning the symbolic language of dreams, a person learns to see what is going on at an unconscious level and what needs to be done about it.

All of us dream. Robert Bosnak claims in *Tracks in the Wilderness of Dreaming,* "If the old research is right, then we're spending seven years of our lives in a constant state of dreaming, in constant creation of this world. And if the new research is right, then we're spending twenty years in that state of dreaming, where world after world is being created." Twenty years of our life. Even seven. How can we not pay attention to our dreams?

How do we do this? How do we listen to our dreams? Let's look first at how Jung did this. How he listened to his dream "Window to Eternity" and understood the dream's symbolic language.

2. Jung's Dream "Window to Eternity"

It was in 1927 that Jung recorded the following dream that was to give confirmation to his ideas about the center and the self. It was and remains an illustration of Jung's achievement.

> *I found myself in a dirty, sooty city. It was night, and winter, dark, and raining. I was in Liverpool. With a number of Swiss, I walked through the dark streets.... We found a broad square dimly illuminated by street lights, into which many streets converged.... In the center was a round pool and in the middle of it a small island. While everything round about was obscured by rain, fog, and dimly lit darkness, the little island blazed with sunlight. On it stood a single tree, a magnolia, in a shower of reddish blossoms. It was as though the tree stood in the sunlight and*

> *were at the same time the source of light.... I was*
> *carried away by the beauty of the flowering tree*
> *and the sunlit island." (MRD, 223)*

In his commentary following the dream, Jung noted that the individual quarters of the city were themselves arranged radially around a center point. This point was the small square with the pool and the island and the magnolia blossom. This radial arrangement was important to him, representing the attraction of the center point.

The dream represented his present situation. He could still see the dull grayish-yellow raincoats of his Swiss colleagues. "Everything was extremely unpleasant, black, and opaque," reflecting how he felt at that moment. Dejected, depressed, disoriented. But he had had this vision of unearthly beauty that gave him reason to continue, reason to live. And it happened in Liverpool, in the "pool of life." There would be a renewal of life-giving energy.

The dream brought with it a sense of finality. Jung saw that he had reached the center. He understood that the goal had been revealed. "One could not go beyond the center. The center is the goal. And everything is directed towards the center." In the center is the archetype of meaning. Jung named this archetype the self. The dream confirmed the development of his thinking during the years that he worked on *The Red Book*. He could now affirm that "the goal of psychic development is the self. There is no linear evolution; there is only a circumambulation of the self." (idem, 222)

Jung was completely satisfied by the dream for it gave a total picture of his situation. Without such a dream, he wrote that he might have lost his orientation. With such a dream, Jung wrote, "one feels it is an act of grace." In listening to the

Window to Eternity, C.G. Jung
Image 159, The Red Book

symbolic language of his dream, he was freed from his depressive thoughts, from the darkness of the streets of Liverpool to the brilliant light of the magnolia tree. The flowering magnolia was an image of the Divine. Jung drew the blossom in the center of one of his last mandalas in 1928. He titled the mandala "Window to Eternity."

We can see the streets leading to the center of the mandala, to the center of Liverpool. We can see the dim streetlights and the dark square in the middle of the city, the round pond, the blossoming magnolia in the very center, lit from within and from without. As we look at the mandala, we enter for a moment into the center, the blossom, into eternity. We are at one with ourselves.

Years later, in writing about the creative process, Jung spoke of shaping an image into a finished work. "By giving it shape, the artist translates it into the present and so makes it possible for us to find our way back to the deepest springs of life." (CW 15, par. 130) In painting his dream in a mandala, Jung had found his way back to the deep springs of life, to the center.

Jung urges us to look at the images of our dreams in this same symbolic way. He invites us to give life to our images through active imagination that I detailed in the preceding chapter. Listening to them, dialoguing with them, drawing them. I write my dreams in my journal, in my one journal, not a separate dream journal. I see them as part of my one life. I write down the dream sometimes in the middle of the night, and then in the morning I write a few comments, what it might be revealing to me. I give the dream a title. I do this slowly, asking myself what is its essence. And I leave a bit of space for more thoughts, for when I go back to the dream and it reveals still more.

A writing suggestion:

Let's remember a dream. What dream comes to you? A recent one, or an old one. Write it down as you remember it. If you are at a loss to remember a dream, let yourself daydream. What image arises? Describe it.

3. Steps to Dreamwork

How do we listen to our dreams? To remember the dream is the first step. If we consciously try to remember our dreams, if we have a pencil and paper near our bedside, if we go to sleep wanting to remember, then remembering will come. When we wake with a dream or a dream image, we need to write it down directly. Even just a sliver. In the morning the sliver will lead us back to the dream. This way, little by little, we will start to remember more of our dreams. How often do we wake with a memory and then it disappears? Gone. We need to tame our dreams to keep them with us. It's like with a pet animal. As we tame it, it comes more willingly to our side.

Once we remember a dream and we have it in writing, the second step is to ask ourselves how we felt about it. Our feelings are clues as to the possible meaning of the dream. Let me give you as an example one of the dreams in my book *Looking for Gold*. First, the dream, titled "Green Frogs," then my feelings and thoughts.

> *I am surrounded by little green frogs, hopping around me happily, maybe ten or fifteen of them. I sit down. There are fewer frogs but they grow bigger. They are now standing on their hind legs, looking at me and still hopping around. I try to catch them. Every time that I get one in my hands,*

71

holding it, a smaller frog pops out, leaving only the old skin in my hands. I try again, but again the frog hops away, leaving the skin behind. And still I try.

I woke up from this dream still trying to hold on to one of the frogs. I could see them, strutting about, almost teasing.... It was winter time, I wondered why I was dreaming about frogs. Frogs were spring time. When I was a little girl, I lived in the countryside outside New York City on a dead-end road with a swamp and fields beyond. Each spring, the peepers in the wet marsh grass would sing, a shrill song which I still identify with my childhood." (83-85)

I continued to write about the dream, how it felt very light and unimportant, especially at a time when I was reading *Faust*. I was reading the Norton Critical Edition of Goethe's *Faust*, one of the longest editions, with 300 pages of verse and another 300 pages of notes. I was clearly becoming inflated with Faust, with his wager with Mephistopheles. I wanted to descend with him into the underworld. When I went to my analyst that week, I did not want to speak about my silly dream; rather I wanted to share my reading of Faust. Keller, my analyst, was not impressed. He nodded and asked, "What about a dream?"

I stop here in my story to underline the importance of this second step of dreamwork: feelings. How did I feel about my dream? I was frustrated, I couldn't catch hold of one of the frogs. They were mocking me. James Hillman writes in *The Dream and the Underworld*, "It is not what is said about the dream after the dream, but the experience of the dream after the dream." *(The Dream and the Underworld,* 122) To experience it anew, I needed to feel it anew. Instead, I wanted to forget it. I had more important things to think about. Keller would prove me wrong.

This brings us to a third step in dreamwork: association. What associations does the dream incur? My dream took me back to my childhood, to the peepers in the swamp at the end of the road where I lived. I could hear them. And on to the present, to my reading of *Faust*. To what was on my mind at that moment. To my wanting to confront Mephistopheles and descend into the underworld. But my analyst was not going there, he wasn't interested, he wanted a dream.

So I shared with Keller my ridiculous little dream. His face lit up immediately and he looked like one of the frogs I couldn't catch. Or did he look like Mephistopheles? I didn't have time to share the comparison. "Look at these frogs," he said. "they jump into the air. They represent the unconscious part of your psyche." (*Looking for Gold*, 85) From treating the associations, we were moving to a deeper level. The frogs were giving me a lesson.

The fourth step would be amplification. Treating the dream image on a symbolic level. The etymology of the word symbol is interesting as it comes from the Greek word *symbolon*, meaning to join what is separated. The ancient Greeks defined *symbolon* as a token identity in the form of a ring, a clay table, or a coin. When friends parted, the ring or coin was broken in half with each friend taking a half as a reminder of their friendship. When the friend returned, the ring or coin was put back together. The friendship was re-established. In dreamwork, we are putting together the two sides of the ring. The dream image on a symbolic level links the visible world with the invisible. We are uniting the conscious mind with the unconscious.

Amplifying an image is like throwing a pebble into the water. When the pebble hits the surface, rings start to circle outward. So in dreamwork we can look at the ripples, following where the image takes us. We can turn to the collective unconscious to find a myth, a fairy tale, song, legend that speaks to the image. The frogs are there, taunting me. Keller suggested that we think about the play *The Frogs* by Aristophanes. In this play, the frogs accompany Dionysus as he travels to the underworld in search of a dead poet. His city is languishing without living poets. I didn't need to catch one of my frogs. Rather, I needed to sit back and let them show me how to live in both the conscious mind and the unconscious. They were there to accompany me into the unconscious. They were images of a new creativity waiting to be born.

After writing down the dream, thinking about feelings, associations, amplification, there is a fifth step to dreamwork that I call animation. Discovering a way to keep the dream alive. Journaling about it, drawing it, finding a physical representation of it. I tried to draw one of the frogs, but it was beyond me. Instead, I found a small dark green ceramic frog and put it in the plant on my kitchen table. When my grandchildren learned about my love of frogs, they started offering me all sorts of frogs—ceramic frogs, glass frogs, bronze frogs, small ones, larger ones, Zen ones, pregnant ones, even a grandmother one. Our house is filled with them. All reminding me to sit back and watch them. Here is one a grandson gave me from when he was studying in China. It is pale green and sits on my desk looking at me.

Here in review are the five suggested steps to working with a dream.

—Remember your dream. Write it down.

—What were your feelings about the dream?

—What associations can you make?

—What amplification can you discover?

—What animation can you create to keep the dream alive?

Green Frog from China

Jung wrote that we work with dream images the same way that nature lets plants grow. "A great work of art is like a dream, it presents an image in the same way as nature allows a plant to grow." (CW 15, par. 160) It is good to remember how plants grow. They are planted in the ground, in the dark. Then to thrive, they need both water and sunshine. Without water and sunshine they die. With too much water, they lose their leaves, their stems shrivel. With too much sunshine, their leaves dry up, their stems waste away. We need to treat our dreams like plants, to go into the dark—the unconscious—to listen and work with them. To water them with our attention and nourish them with our creativity. And to not give them too much cerebral sunshine!

Before the next section, think about the dream you wrote and how to work with it. Start with your feelings. Bring the dream back to life.

A writing suggestion:

Read anew your dream and think about the different steps. What are your feelings? Does it bring up any associations? Write down a few notes.

4. Writing from Dreams

We have listened to dreams; now let's turn to writing from dreams. How do we write life stories from a dream? As dreams take us deeper into our imagination, we begin to imagine their stories. We can write a story in a myriad of ways: journal entry, personal essay, page of a memoir, short story, page of a novel, folk tale or fable, prose poem or poem. In *Looking for Gold,* I wrote about many of the dreams I had during my first year of analysis. Each chapter begins with a dream; one was about my green frogs. Other images were cat at the door, murky water, witch in the yard, maple tree, windmills and pigs, trapeze act, pieces of gold. The dreams became chapters in my memoir, followed by how I relived them, how they opened the way to an encounter with the unconscious.

The book itself came from a dream. I was at a writers conference for the International Women's Writing Guild in upstate New York. I had just finished one year of Jungian analysis and was talking enthusiastically to other writers about where it was taking me. I woke in the middle of the night with the title and chapters of this book clear in my mind. I'd call it *Looking for Gold*. The alchemical gold within. Each chapter would treat a dream image. I had never considered writing nonfiction. I was writing a novel. But there it was. A book about my analysis and how it awakened my creativity. I wrote

76

down the dream before going back to sleep. I still have it in my notebooks. Confirmation that such dreams happen.

When I was back in Geneva, I took the idea to Keller. He said, "Go with it." So for one year, I wrote about dreams. Was this fiction or nonfiction? Certainly the dreams, the analysis, the life experiences were mine, making it nonfiction. But at the same time, it was so much how I imagined it that it was also fiction, in a way that Hermes, the Trickster God, might well recognize. I gave the manuscript to Keller to read. When he returned it, he alleged, "If you had asked your unconscious for a good story, it couldn't have given you a better one."

Let's look at other writers who have written from their dreams. I turn to the book *Writers Dreaming*.

Writers Dreaming

In this book, the editor Naomi Epel interviews writers about the role of dreams in their work and lets the writers speak for themselves. Epel was interested in dream writing and was leading workshops to help people tap into their hidden creativity. When she began asking writers about their dreams she had no idea a book was in the making. There would follow fascinating conversations. But it wasn't until she herself had a dream that the project for this book took hold and became a reality.

In this dream Epel is standing in a doorway watching an artist who is working in a basement room. Somehow she knows that he does not want to be disturbed. But she knows also that if she remains quiet, he will let her stay. In relating the dream to a friend the next morning, she found herself in tears. She experienced how good it felt to just be quiet and watch the artist. She realized that the dream was telling her to stop all her busy work and activities. To be quiet and listen to the artist in her basement. And so it was that her inner artist took her by hand and led her to compose the book, *Writers Dreaming*.

She opens the Introduction to her book with this description of how William Styron dreamed the opening of his book *Sophie's Choice*.

> *One morning in the spring of 1974 William Styron woke to the lingering image of a woman he had known in his early twenties. He could see her standing in a hallway, her arms full of books, the blue numbers of a tattoo visible beneath her sleeve. Suddenly he knew it was time to tell this woman's story. He went directly to his studio and wrote the opening paragraphs of what was to become Sophie's Choice. (Writers Dreaming, 1)*

Styron, in one of Epel's last interviews, explains that he had been slaving away on a book that was not coming together. He was getting more and more upset over the fact that his writing was not proceeding well. Then one morning he woke with this lingering vision, a merging from the dream to a conscious memory of this girl named Sophie. It was so powerful that he knew he was going to abandon the other book and write the story of Sophie.

A dream image leading to a story. This experience is repeated throughout the pages of *Writers Dreaming* as the different authors describe how their dreams open the doors to the worlds of their imagination. In relating the way they transform their dreams into art, the writers provide insights into their creative process and the craft of writing. Insights which reveal the role of their inner artist.

Let's turn here to three of the writers that Naomi Epel interviewed—Maya Angelou, Stephen King, and Reynold

Price—and to their observations which are written in their own words.

Maya Angelou

In her interview, Maya Angelou speaks about a dream that she delights in, a dream that means her writing is going well or that her writing will go well. She dreams of a very tall building which is being built with scaffolds and staircases and steps. She is climbing them with eagerness and joy and laughter. She keeps climbing. And she writes, "I just can't tell you how delicious that is!" Whenever she gets that dream, she knows her work is going to be all right for the next weeks.

Concerning the role of dreams in her creative process, Angelou writes, "Dreams can tell people all sorts of things. They can work out problems. Especially for writing." (idem, 30) Sometimes when a writer is stuck and is hesitant to get to a new depth in a fictional character, the brain says, "Okay, you go on and go to sleep, I'll take care of it. I'll show you." And the brain does so, allowing the dreamer to do things, consider things and go places that in real time, the person would never do.

At the end of her interview, Angelou shares that there is a phrase in West Africa called 'deep talk.' When a person learns about a situation, an older person will often use a parable, adding to it, 'take that as deep talk.' She writes that you may never find the answer. "Dreams may be deep talk." (ibid.)

Stephen King

The author, Stephen King writes, "One of the things that I've been able to use dreams for in my stories is to show things in a symbolic way that I wouldn't want to come right out and say directly." (idem, 134) Dreams are a way that people's minds illustrate in symbolic language the nature of their life experiences, maybe even illustrating the answers to their problems, in symbolic language.

Part of his function as a writer is to dream awake. King explains that if he sits down in the morning to write, he is aware that he is writing at his desk in the beginning of the session and in the ending of the session. But in the middle, the desk and the world around him disappear, they are no longer there, and he is able to see more clearly, write more clearly. If you are able, he writes, to put yourself in that semi-dreaming state, you can remember things that you thought you had forgotten. Creative imaging and dreaming, King believes, are so similar that they must be related.

He appreciates how precious that state is, and the ability to go there when one is awake. It's a bit like finding a secret door into a room without knowing how he got there. He does not remember the first time he found that state except that he was sitting down to write every day, pretty much at the same time. And this "seems to be a way of saying to the mind: you're going to be dreaming soon." (idem, 142)

Reynold Price

The poet, Reynold Price, has taken dreams seriously almost all of his conscious life. Even in childhood he was aware of his dreams and found them scary. Then in his early adult years, he took them as clues to his psychic life. Once he started writing full time, dreams began to feed into his work. Sometimes when working intensely on a book and on a particular character, he would find himself with dreams that seemed more appropriate to the character than to himself. He would literally transcribe them into his writing as coming from the character.

In his three books of poetry, he has several poems called the dream of so and so, "The Dream of a House," "The

Dream of Food," "The Dream of Lee." Each time these are instances of when he woke up in the morning with a fascinating dream, not the usual boring kind, "but something that was a wonderful story in itself, that I thought anybody could enjoy reading." (idem, 202) So he would sit down and write it as a straight-forward poem, wanting to preserve the wonderful story of the dream.

He closes his interview saying that he stays informed of the latest theories of sleep and dreaming but that he is old-fashioned enough to think that a lot of times our dreams are attempts on the part of our brain to communicate a discovery to us. "Either, you'd better *stop* doing so and so; or you'd better *do* so and so." And this was how an old dream of his, ten years before his surgery, revealed that his brain was perceiving his cancer years before the doctor found it.

It is the dream he turned into the poem, "the Dream of a House", without thinking that the eerie story of finding a human corpse hanging up in a clothes closet would be his darkest secret, that he had a malignant tumor hanging up in his spine. Confined to a wheelchair, Reynold Price continued to dream and to write for the last 27 years of his life.

Let us return to editor Naomi Epel who in exploring the ways these writers transform their dreams into art, unearths the raw materials with which they create their work. She writes in the Introduction that her book is not only about writing, but also about the affects dreams have on a writer's personal life. That in talking about their dreams, they reveal their fears, desires and anxieties.

Here is the ending of her introduction.

I hope that this intimate glimpse behind the scenes into these writers' minds will be both enlightening and inspiring—granting you fresh

> *insight into the creative process, increased*
> *understanding of your own dreams and a rich*
> *relationship with the artist in your basement.*
> *(idem, 6)*

It is through dreaming, and writing from our dreams, that we nourish this relationship with our inner artist. We may not wake up with the image from a dream as William Styron did and rush to our desk to start writing a best-selling novel, but if we hold on to the image, our inner artist will take our hand and lead us to a story.

In so doing, the veil between our conscious mind and our dreaming mind will be lifted. We will be in that space where our writing desk disappears and we see more clearly. As Jung wrote, our dreams are little hidden doors "opening into the cosmic night of the unconscious." In writing from our dreams, we get a glimpse into a deeper life, below the surface of our everydayness. We take a step toward wholeness.

It's now your turn to listen anew to your dream and write from it. You have held on to an image from it, you have thought about associations. Now let the artist in your own basement take your hand and lead you to a story.

A writing suggestion:
Return to your dream and let it lead you to an experience in your life. Write about the experience, it's your story.

In conclusion, I turn to the dream that Jung had in his student years.

> *It was night in some unknown place and I was*
> *making slow and painful headway against a*
> *mighty wind. Dense fog was flying everywhere.*

I had my hands cupped around a tiny light which threatened to go out at any moment. Everything depended on my keeping this little light alive. Suddenly I had the feeling that something was coming up behind me. I looked back and saw a gigantic black figure following me." (MDR, 107-08)

In spite of his terror, he was conscious that he must keep his little light burning through night and wind. When he woke, he realized that the gigantic figure was his own shadow on the swirling mists. He knew also that this little light was his consciousness, the only light he has, his sole treasure. He will go forward with his shadow against the storm, keeping the light of his consciousness burning at all costs.

This is the light within each of us, the light that we take into the world around us, into the whirling winds of darkness, the light that we can hold high to lighten the way for others. The light is nourished by all that we do to bridge the world of consciousness and the world of the unconscious. Our dreams show us the way.

Chapter Four

Composing Metaphor: Illuminating Lives

"An archetypal content expresses itself first
and foremost in metaphors."
C.G. Jung

"Imagination is more important than knowledge."
Einstein

What is metaphor? What is its role in our lives? In this chapter we will first look at the meaning of metaphor and how it has been used in world cultures over the centuries. We will explore how C.G. Jung used metaphor and why *The Red Book* has been called a metaphorical soul quest, examining excerpts from both *The Red Book* and *Memories, Dreams, Reflections*. We will then look at how metaphor is used in the work of contemporary writer, Annie Dillard, and in my own work, to discern how it can inform our writing and our way of being.

1. Defining Metaphor

Metaphor is not language but an idea expressed in language. The word comes from the 16th-century French *metaphore,* coming from the Latin *metaphora* (carrying over) and from the Greek *metaphorá* (also to carry over). We see the prefix *meta* meaning after, across, beyond, and the word *phero* meaning to bear, to carry. Hence, the connotation, to carry beyond. Metaphor carries beyond. The etymology of the word gives us the evocative meaning of a journey beyond.

Aristotle wrote, "Metaphor is the application of a word to one thing that belongs to another thing." (*Poetics*, written 335 B.C.E.). It was seen as a rhetorical device in which the traits of one thing are attributed to something else. Over the centuries, its usage has been extended, and metaphor has become a component of meaning in human expression where one part of human experience is used to illuminate another, to hint at a deeper meaning.

If we look at lines from Shakespeare's *As You Like It,* here is first a metaphor used as a figure of speech, transferring a word from one context to another. "All the world's a stage..." The subject is the world. The attribute is a stage. The word "world" is transferred from the context of the universe to the context of a theater. Now if we look at the next line: "And all the men and women merely players; / They have their exits and their entrances," the metaphor is expanded. Not only is the world a stage, but the men and women are merely players, their lives are transitory. The metaphor reveals a new dimension of reality, a new dimension of truth. We are reminded of our own entrances and exits, of our human frailty.

As such, metaphor permeates our sense of reality and leads to an associative way of being. In a way, it is no longer this or that, but this *and* that. Things are no longer all black or all white. We revise our way of thinking, our way of perceiving the world. We become aware of our creative capacity to see the world anew. According to Nietzsche we are in metaphor or we are metaphor. Our being is derived not uniquely from a Platonic essence or a Cartesian thinking substance, but from the interactions of several different perspectives. Truth is, again Nietzsche, "a movable host of metaphors."

To avoid confusion with similar terms, here is a list of words that express like meaning and with short definitions of each.

—simile: the comparison of two unlike things, with words like or as. (She is like a budding rose.)

—metaphor: the description of one thing as something else. (She is a budding rose.)

—analogy: the comparison between one thing and another.

—allegory: an extended metaphor in which a story illustrates an attribute of the subject.

—parable: an extended metaphor in which a story teaches a moral lesson.

—myth: an extended metaphor in which the story had cultural connotations.

—symbol: the relationship of something to something deeper, often generated by metaphors.

We note here the closeness of meaning between symbol and metaphor in how they are used. Both take us to a new understanding. However symbol carries the metaphor to a hitherto unknown level of meaning. As James Hollis underlines in his book *The Archetypal Imagination*, metaphor is something that will "carry over from one thing to another", and symbol is something that will "project toward convergence." (4)

Definitions are always problematic. We will stay with metaphor meaning the description of one thing as something else. And we will appreciate how it is used to reveal a new dimension of perception. As we review the place of metaphor in literature throughout the centuries, we will see how it effectively deepens the way we perceive ourselves and the world around us.

2. Metaphor in Literature over the Centuries

Metaphor was present in our oldest known written narrative, *The Epic of Gilgamesh*. The unnamed author used metaphor to illuminate the legendary life of Gilgamesh, a semi-mythic demigod of superhuman strength. As noted in Chapter Three, Jung gives Gilgamesh in *The Red Book* the name of Izdubar, the pagan God coming from the East whom Jung encounters in his travels in the underworld. Scholars today believe that Gilgamesh was a historical king of Uruk in Babylonia, the modern Iraq. He lived around 2700 B.C.E. Numerous myths were written about him. The fullest surviving version was found on stone tablets in the ruins of the library of the King of Assyria.

Here are a few lines from Tablet VIII where metaphor brings to light Gilgamesh's love for his soul brother Enkidu and his heartbreak over Enkidu's death.

Enkidu, my friend, the swift mule, fleet wild ass of the mountain, panther of the wilderness, after we joined together and went up into the mountain, fought the Bull of Heaven and killed it, now what is this sleep that has seized you?

By the use of metaphor—swift mule, fleet wild ass, panther of the wilderness—the author gives us a visual picture of Enkidu, revealing both how Gilgamesh saw him and how deeply he appreciated him. We learn also how Gilgamesh envisaged death, as a deep sleep that seized without warning his companion.

Advancing through the centuries, there is "The Song of Songs," a beautiful portrayal of the mutual love of Yahweh and his people through metaphor. First thought to be a love song between Solomon and the Queen of Sheba, it is also known as the Song of Solomon. However, it was most likely written centuries after King Solomon, sometime between 900 B.C.E. and 200 B.C.E. The Lord is the lover, and his people are the beloved. It is likewise possible to see it as a poetic portrayal of the love of the Lord and the individual soul. Lover and beloved.

Extending the metaphor, we can see it as an erotic portrayal of human love. Several scholars believe this was its original intent.

> *Let him kiss me with the kisses of his mouth....*
> *As a lily among the thistles, so is my love among*
> *the maidens.*
> *As an apple tree among the trees of the orchard,*
> *so is my beloved among the young men. (Jeru-*
> *salem Bible, pp.865-866)*

Through the use of images from nature as metaphors, the author magnifies the sheer power and beauty of love—between the Lord and his people, between the Lord and the individual soul, between two human beings.

Next, we look at one of the best-known metaphors, known as the Myth of the Cave, found in Plato's *The Republic,* 380 B.C.E. Written as a dialogue between Plato's teacher Socrates and Plato's brother Glaucon, Plato attributes the metaphor of the cave to our habitat. We live imprisoned in a cave, blind to reality. He extends the metaphor, to show how we see only the shadows of living forms, not the beings themselves. Imagine a group of people who live enchained in a cave, facing a blank wall. All they see are shadows projected onto the wall by beings passing behind them in front of a fire. It is only the philosopher, who is freed from the chains, who can perceive the true form of reality. The rest of us remain enchained and see only the shadows of reality.

*Here they have been from childhood, chained by
the leg and also by the neck, so that they cannot
move and can see only what is in front of them....
Prisoners so confined would have seen nothing
of themselves or of one another, except the
shadows thrown by the fire light on the wall of
the cave facing them. (Plato, The Republic, Book
VII, 514-516)*

Moving into the Common Era, it is interesting to
compare the metaphors in the New Testament with those in
the Quran. Both Jesus and Muhammad taught in parables,
using metaphor to teach a moral lesson. When asked why he
taught in parables, Jesus replied, "The reason I talk to them
in parables is that they look without seeing and listen without
hearing...but happy are your eyes because they see, your ears
because they hear!" (Mat. 13:16) Muhammad would teach the
same lesson.

Here are a few lines from Mark 4:1

*Listen! Imagine a sower going out to sow. Now
it happened that as he sowed, some of the seed
fell on the edge of the path...some seed fell on
rocky ground...some seed fell into thorns.... And
some seeds fell into rich soil and growing tall
and strong, produced crop; and yielded thirty,
sixty, even a hundredfold. (The Jerusalem Bible,
50)*

And in the Quran, 2:265

*The likeness of those who expend their wealth
for the cause of God, is that of a grain of corn
which produceth seven ears, and in each ear a
hundred grains...is as a garden on a hill, on*

90

> *which the heavy rain falleth, and it yieldeth its*
> *fruits twofold; and even if a heavy rain fall not*
> *on it, yet is there a dew: God beholdeth your*
> *actions. (The Koran, 29)*

The two teachers are using similar metaphors, taken from the daily life around them, to instruct their followers. The believer is likened to a seed, to a grain that yields twofold or a hundredfold. God is likened to the sower who "beholdeth your actions."

In the 12ᵗʰ century, we come to Hildegard of Bingen, Benedictine Abbess, cited in earlier chapters, who used extended metaphors to describe the visions that held her enthralled from her early years. It was only at the age of 40, that she shared her visions, illustrating them with drawings on wax tablets. In Hildegard's *Book of Divine Works*, Vision Four "On the Articulation of the Body," titled "Cultivating the Cosmic Tree" by Mathew Fox, exemplifies her use of metaphor.

Here, Hildegard sees the entire creation, the entire universe, as a circle. She draws it in a mandala, with circles of light, water, fire, air, and the inner sphere—the earth with its cosmic tree—circling around the center. Hildegard situates humankind here in the inner sphere as the gardeners of the creation, tending the tree through the seasons of the year.

The universe is seen as a circle, a mandala, each element—light, water, fire, air, earth—another smaller circle. And the tree of life, tended by humankind, circling around the center. In the picture, she draws herself in the left-hand corner, etching the vision onto a wax tablet.

> *The firmament follows a circular orbit as a*
> *metaphor of God's might, which has neither*
> *beginning nor end and no one can tell where the*

Cultivating the Cosmic Tree, Hildegard of Bingen

circular wheel begins or ends. God's throne is
the divine eternity, and all living creatures are
sparks from the radiation of God's brilliance.
(Book of Divine Works, 86)

The metaphorical language uplifts us. The creation is a vast beautiful mandala, a metaphor of God's might. We are sparks from the radiance of God's brilliance.

Four centuries later, Shakespeare deftly uses metaphor as we have seen earlier in his play *As You Like It.* Here, let's look at a sonnet. He wrote 154 sonnets, mostly addressed to a mysterious lover, first published in a 1609 Quarto. Perhaps the most famous is Sonnet 18,

Shall I compare thee to a summer's day?
Thou art more lovely and more temperate:

Shakespeare illustrates the comparison with images from nature, the darling buds of May, rough winds, the hot eye of heaven, and concludes,

So long as men can breathe or eyes can see,
So long lives this, and this gives life to thee.

The metaphors are multiple. Shakespeare is comparing the woman or friend he loves to a beautiful summer day. And yet a summer's day is threatened by rough winds, and summer's lease is short. Life moves on, but the poet has assured immortality to the person he loves through the writing of his poem.

Having considered this selective overview of how metaphor has been used throughout the centuries and before looking at how it is used in the work of C.G. Jung, let's find a few metaphors ourselves.

A writing suggestion:

If you close your eyes, what image appears? Describe it in a couple of lines. Think now about a metaphor. What can you compare it to? Play with the comparison. Where does it take you?

3. Metaphor in C.G. Jung's *Memories, Dreams, Reflections* and *The Red Book*

So much has been written and studied about metaphors and symbols in C.G. Jung's work that I limit myself here to the topic of composing metaphor in our quest for wholeness. We noted earlier that metaphors and symbols are very close in how they are used, both describing one thing as something else, yet with symbol leading to an unknown something. Murray Stein wrote in *Minding the Self*, "Symbols may resemble metaphors, even though they surpass them in depth and spiritual significance." (28) Let us first look at a few examples from *Memories, Dreams, Reflections* before turning to *The Red Book,* for examples of how Jung worked with his metaphors, how he looked for their symbolic significance.

In the Prologue to *Memories, Dreams, Reflections*, Jung sees life like a plant that lives on its rhizome. He is here using a simile to compare life to a plant. He continues the comparison: "Its true life is invisible, hidden in the rhizome. That part that appears above ground lasts only a single summer." The simile deepens into metaphor. "Then it withers away—an ephemeral apparition." Life above ground is ephemeral. But underground, something lives. The metaphor is taking on symbolic significance. "I have never lost a sense of something that lives and endures underneath the eternal flux. What we see is the blossom which passes. The rhizome remains." (*MDR*, 18)

This word "rhizome" continues to speak to me. Recently when reading again *Memories, Dreams, Reflections*, the blossoms and the rhizome called out to me to be pictured, to be drawn in my journal. Here is my pencil drawing. The tendrils in the earth reach out from the drawing.

Rhizome

Throughout the first chapters—"First Years," "School Years," "Student Years"—Jung thinks back to his early memories and gives them metaphorical expression. The blue sky and golden sunlight above his pram revealed not only the glorious beauty of the day but gave him, as a very young child, a sense of well-being. Everything was wholly wonderful. As he grows older, he sees earthly manifestations of God's world in the realm of plants. Trees in particular were direct embodiments of the incomprehensible meaning of life. He could imagine himself peering over the shoulder of the Creator who was decorating the world.

Then in his student years, there was his widening rift with his father and with his father's entrapment in the theological thinking of the Protestant Church. His mother's No. 2 personality offered him support between paternal tradition and "the strange compensatory products" from his unconscious. And after his father's death, during his university studies, the Holy Ghost became a metaphor for the God he could not believe in or conceive.

His autobiography continues—"Psychiatric Activities," "Sigmund Freud," "Confrontation with the Unconscious," "The Work"—and the rendering continues to be metaphorical. Jung is looking always for the invisible meaning underneath what he is living. Looking for the rhizome. We arrive at the chapter titled, "The Tower." As his own individuation continues, so the tower represents the stages of his own growth. The first tower, the middle section, and then after his wife's death in 1955, the upper story representing himself. This last addition signified an extension of consciousness attained in old age. We will see the Tower as a metaphor for Jung's psychic development in greater detail in Chapter Eight.

As Jung writes about his travels and visions, and then the chapters "Life After Death" and "Late Thoughts," he continues to have recourse to metaphor. In relating the story of his life, in defining his myth, Jung uncovers and returns without cease to "the presence of an apparently universal symbol of a similar type—the mandala symbol." (idem, 367) This circular image represents "the wholeness of the self." To put it in mythic terms, Jung sees the mandala as representing "the divinity incarnate in man." Jung here gives us in metaphorical language his numinous God image, the divinity incarnate in man, the Self. (I use here a capital S as I am specifically referring to the self as a God image.)

I turn now back to *The Red Book,* looking to appreciate how through metaphor Jung uncovered the deep meaning of the visions that nearly overwhelmed him during his confrontation with the unconscious. As I wrote in the first chapter, Jung's journey began after his break with Freud in November 1913, when at the height of his acclaimed career, he found himself in a period of inner confusion and realized he had lost his way. He had lost his soul. Overwhelmed by a twice-repeated vision of a monstrous flood covering northern Europe, he wrestled with its possible meaning. Then the world war broke out, a monstrous flood of blood covered Europe, and he realized that his own experience coincided with that of mankind in general. Let us look here at how Jung first wrestled with the vision, committing himself to understanding its meaning.

> *When I had the vision of the flood in October of the year 1913, it happened at a time that was significant for me as a man. At that time, in the fortieth year of my life, I had achieved every-thing I had wished for myself.... The vision of the flood seized me and I felt the spirit of the depths but I did not understand him. Yet he drove me on with unbearable inner longing. (Refinding the Soul, The Red Book, 231)*

So it is that Jung sets out to confront his unconscious. Throughout *The Red Book,* Jung notes his encounters as metaphors. He calls out to his soul, "Who are you child?" seeing the soul as a young maiden. He loses himself in a desert with an unbearably hot sun, the sun representing his consciousness. He compares his soul to a tree and longs to sit in its shade. He meets Elijah, the Old Testament prophet, representing logos, and Salome, the dancer who asked for John the Baptist's head, representing eros. In *The Red Book*, Salome is blind, extending the metaphor to show how underdeveloped was this side in Jung's personality.

The encounters continue, he banters with the Red Knight representing the devil who soon reveals himself as the personification of joy. He meets Izdubar, the pagan god Gilgamesh, embodying Eastern philosophy while he embodies Western science. From this encounter is born finally a new image of God. And then Philemon, the magician, the husband of Baucis in Ovid's recounting of the myth. I am skipping through the pages in order to show the multitude of metaphors that await the reader of *The Red Book*.

Let's look at one of these metaphors, one encounter in detail that follows closely upon Jung's dialogues with his soul in the desert, the encounter with Elijah and his daughter Salome—Elijah the prophet and Salome the dancer. We understand Jung's bewilderment, father and daughter? Elijah and Salome? How can this be?

> *An old man stood before me. He looked like one of the old prophets. A black serpent lay at his feet. Some distance away I saw a house with columns. A beautiful maiden steps out of the door. She walks uncertainly and I see that she is blind. The old man waves to me and I follow him to the house.... The serpent creeps behind us. Darkness reigns inside the house. We are in a high hall with glittering walls. A bright stone the color of water lies in the background....*
>
> *We step outside and the old man says to me, "Do you know where you are?"*

I: "I am a stranger here and everything seems strange to me, anxious as in a dream. Who are you?"

E: "I am Elijah and this is my daughter Salome."

I: "The daughter of Herod, the bloodthirsty woman?"

E: "Why do you judge so? You see that she is blind. She is my daughter, the daughter of the prophet."

I: "What miracle has united you?"

E: "It is no miracle, it was so from the beginning. My wisdom and my daughter are one."

I: "How could it be that this unholy woman and you, the prophet of your God, could be one?"

E: "Why are you amazed: But you see it, we are together."

I: "What my eyes see is exactly what I cannot grasp.... You are the symbol of the most extreme contradiction."

E. "We are real and not symbols." (Mysterium Encounter, idem, 245-46)

This is one of the longest encounters in *The Red Book*. Jung called it the mystery play, the Mysterium, and described as the coming together of logos and eros. In the Commentary that follows the vision, Jung perceives Elijah as the thinking person and Salome as the feeling person. One is thought-bound, the other pleasure-bound. He writes: "May the thinking person accept his pleasure and the feeling person accept his own thought. Such leads one along the way." (idem, 248) We see here how by addressing the figures in his vision, putting them on the stage and creating a mystery play—the practice that Jung named active imagination—Jung is led to defining the psychological functions of thinking and feeling.

There are other metaphors in the above passage, the dark house where Elijah and Salome live, the darkness of the unconscious. And yet there are the glittering walls, light in the darkness. And the blue stone could be a foreshadowing of the alchemical lapis, the Philosopher's Stone, that Jung draws in a beautiful mandala later on his journey.

There remains the serpent who will accompany Jung as he continues his journey. Already in the opening page of *The Red Book*, and first illustration, the drawing of the letter D, there is the serpent rising out of a pot of fire, representing the energy that would lead Jung forward. The serpent as a metaphor of the earthly essence will take on deeper meaning, sometimes black, sometimes white. And Jung extends its writhing to represent human life. "The way of life writhes like the serpent from right to left and from left to right, from thinking to pleasure and from pleasure to thinking." (idem, 247)

Later in his journey, Jung again befriends the serpents in the Magician's garden. He plays his flute to one of them, to make her believe she is his soul. Her words are soothing. She asks him if he has noticed that his approach to the soul follows a serpentine path. "How soon day becomes night, and night day." Jung listens closely. His serpent soul is communicating her wisdom to him.

If we recall Jung's words to Christiana Morgan in 1926 advising her to write everything down in her journal which will become her church, her cathedral, we can see the entire *Red Book* as a magnificent metaphor for Jung's cathedral. As we enter it, reading the first pages, we are entering Jung's church, a mandala in the center, the altar, a metaphor for the Self, for Jung's image of God. The stained-glass windows portray the different figures of his imagination: Elijah, Salome, the snake, the Red Knight, the white bird, Izdubar,

Philemon. The liturgies are his ongoing dialogues with each of the imagined figures. We are inside Jung's cathedral.

Jung has found his way, and he invites us to find our way. To enter into our own unconscious and speak with the image that is waiting there for us. Then to write it down in our own red books.

A writing suggestion:

Return to the image that you wrote about and ask it why it has come to you. What does it want to tell you? Wait for an answer. Write the conversation as a dialogue.

4. Metaphor in Contemporary Literature

Annie Dillard

I turn now to a contemporary author, to Annie Dillard, who uses metaphor extensively to illuminate the meaning in her stories. Annie Dillard sees the natural world as a radiant metaphor of the spirit. Her work as a writer, as a human being, is to keep an eye on things. She writes that we are born to witness. In *Teaching a Stone to Talk,* a collection of 14 personal essays, she asks herself how does one face a world of silent stones? It is by touching the mystery of nature, by feeling the hushing pulse of a total eclipse, by seeing the *palo santo* trees crowding the cliff sides of the Galapagos.

Dillard embraces the essay form, saying that it gives the metaphor room to expand. The poet must compress his or her metaphors sometimes to a few lines. The essayist in devoting pages to a narrative or to expanded reflections and description can more vividly bring forth the meaning of the metaphor.

This is what Dillard does in her essay "A Field of Silence." Dillard is writing here about silence. She locates her essay in a place called "the farm," where she once lived. Its flat messy pastures ran along one side of a quarter-mile road on an island in Puget Sound on the Washington coast. From the farm she could see eastward across the water to the mainland and still further to the mountains coated with snow. The farm seemed eternal, as old as earth itself. She lived there once and saw the roadside pastures stacked with silence.

I saw the silence heaped on the fields like trays.
That day the green hayfields supported silence
evenly sown; the fields bent just so under the
even pressure of silence, bearing it, palming it
aloft: cleared fields, part of a land, that did not
buckle beneath the heel of silence, nor split up
scattered to bits but instead lay secret, disguised
as time and matter as though that were nothing.
(Teaching a Stone to Talk, 131)

This is striking to see silence heaped like trays. Silence evenly sown, layered in the fields like trays. A simile. Then fields bent under its even pressure. Fields that bent to bear the silence and to palm it aloft. A metaphor, fields not buckled beneath the heel of silence. The metaphor expands.

Several months later, walking past the farm, Dillard remarked to a friend, "There are angels in those fields." Angels! She writes that she had rarely been so surprised by something she said. Until that moment, she had never thought of angels, not at all.

From that time I began to think of angels…. My
impression now of those fields is of thousands of

> *spirits…angels in fact, almost discernible to the*
> *eye, and whirling. If pressed I would say they*
> *were three or four feet from the ground….*
>
> *There are angels in those fields, and I*
> *presume, in all fields, and everywhere else.*
> *(idem, 135-136)*

Dillard now presumes that there are angels in heaps of silence everywhere. She has moved from fields of silence to thousands of angels, whirling, three or four feet from the ground. Her metaphor has literally taken wings. And she delightfully ends her essay writing that she would go to the lions to witness this fact.

Susan Tiberghien

I give one more example of the use of metaphor in writing, this time from my book, *Looking for Gold, A Year in Jungian Analysis.* I am speaking here of the alchemical gold, the sparks of divinity that are within all of us. Each chapter unfolds from a dream during my first year of analysis. In writing the book, I uncovered what was to become a dominant metaphor in my life, the crack in my water jug. It would appear in all my subsequent books.

Here is the story as I explained it during my first visit to an analyst in Geneva. I had related to her the previous night's dream in which I was going somewhere to have my shoulder fixed. The dream was long, with many visual details. She asked about my shoulder and said what was important was the crack. Her words flustered me. Yes, there was a crack in my shoulder. But there was another crack more recent from a car accident. I was driving home from a day at the monastery in Les Voirons, mountains close to Geneva.

> *I was driving back home when a bee flew into the car. Instead of stopping, I tried to kill it and, distracted, I drove right into a cliff. I turned over twice and pulled myself out of the wreck, picking up the water jug I had bought at the monastery— an earthenware jug, pottery which the sisters made, wrapped in a single sheet of newspaper. An ambulance carried me to the hospital at Geneva. I was not hurt nor was the jug. The car was finished.*
>
> *Then with time a crack started to appear on the jug, a fine line etching its way onto the smooth gray surface. I wrote a story about the water jug, explaining how the crack was within, making the jug vulnerable. (Looking for Gold, 19)*

The analyst stopped me and said that it would be through this crack that I would enter and go deeper. She added that it might hurt. I was brought up short to think of my shoulder hurting me anew. I had learned to live with it. Here was the crack in my water jug revealing the crack in my shoulder. Metaphors revealing synchronicity. Yes, I would enter the crack.

Ever since, as I continue to enter the crack, I see it defining me, making me vulnerable. Inviting me to enter more deeply into the dark, into the unconscious. And at the same time inviting me to reveal my crack, to show my vulnerability. To open myself to those I encounter and to the light. The jug now rests on our kitchen table. In the morning as I sit down to breakfast and look at it, I ask myself, how will I live today? How will I show my vulnerability? How will I let more light into the darkness within me? The metaphor of the water jug and its crack continues to transform the way I see myself, the way I see the world.

Crack in the Water Jug

I continue to write about it. Here I express its lesson in a prose poem as written in my book *Footsteps, In Love with a Frenchman.*

The Crack

In the monastery on top of Mont Voirons, the little sister turned the earthenware jug, one ring at a time in silence. Her hands shaped the long spiral of dark gray clay from wide circles at the bottom into smaller circles at the top. Slowly she smoothed the still moist surface, cupping her hands in prayer around the jug.

Only later, many years later, did the crack appear, climbing upward through the rings of

105

> *clay. Like a fine vein, it etched itself on the smooth surface, coming from deep within, from the silence of its creator. (129)*

In leaving the "its creator" undefined, I expand the metaphor of the crack climbing upward through rings of clay to hint at the silence of creation. As I am vulnerable, so is the little sister, so is the creation.

In these examples, the metaphors are used to add a component of meaning to the story. The metaphor of angels representing silence for Annie Dillard becomes a way to bear witness. And in my work, the crack in the water jug becomes a way to open myself to the light.

As in Jung's writing in *Memories, Dreams, Reflections* and in *The Red Book,* the use of metaphor enables us to live simultaneously in two worlds, the visible and the invisible. Through comparison, metaphor opens the way to discovering the deeper meaning of what we are experiencing, of what we are writing about.

Before concluding this chapter, I suggest that you write the story of the image you have been working with. Let it open the door to a new perception about your life.

A writing suggestion:

Focus anew on the image that called to you, that you described and with whom you dialogued. Befriend it and write its story.

Jung's journey was metaphorical, wherein each new experience took him deeper into the unknown. As he wrote down the visions—describing the figures, dialoguing with them, commenting on the encounters—and copied them into the large leather-bound Red Book, with artwork and magnificent paintings, *The Red Book* became his cathedral, the silent place of his spirit. This is what we wish to do with our own journal entries, to create our own cathedrals.

In so doing, we can imagine ourselves creating one vast cathedral for humanity. Millions of workers, millions of makers, building one universal cathedral. Whatever we uncover in our own forays into the unconscious, whatever images we bring alive, whatever metaphors we create, all of this contributes to humanity's journey to wholeness.

Chapter Five

Seeing Beauty with Words: Awakening the Soul

"Give me beauty in the inward soul.
May the outward and inner man be at one."
Socrates

"To see a world in a grain of sand / And heaven in a wild flower."
Blake

"Whenever we awaken beauty, we are helping to make
God present in the world."
O'Donohue

From Socrates to Blake to O'Donohue, beauty has been seen as a doorway to the spiritual world. In contemplating beauty, we awaken our soul. We lift our wings, as it were. In this lesson we will follow on the paths of poets, writers, and mystics as they celebrate beauty. They will show us the way to let beauty open our hearts and minds to the Eternal.

First, we will look at how beauty has been honored throughout the centuries, from the hymns to Inanna in 3000 B.C.E. to the journals of Thomas Merton and the writings of John O'Donohue in our time. We will then turn to C.G. Jung to lead us deeper in our quest for beauty, to appreciate its impact on Jung's own soul. And to Simone Weil, who saw beauty as the portal to the realm of the transcendent. We will read excerpts from both of their works.

Lastly, we will add our own voices to those of a few contemporary authors, Terry Tempest Williams and Marion Woodman, to celebrate together the gift of beauty, knowing that when we honor and protect beauty around us, we honor and protect beauty in the entire universe.

The Love of Beauty Throughout the Centuries

In ancient times, the love of beauty surrounded the whole of life with wondrous poetry. Beauty was revered, be it in human form, both feminine and masculine, or in the natural world, the silver moon, the blossoming hyacinth. Very often the two converged. All creation was to be revered as a metaphor for beauty. And beauty was seen as the manifestation of the Divine.

Let us go back to the hymns sung to Inanna, Goddess of Love and Beauty, worshipped in Sumer in the fourth millennium. Her name comes from the Sumerian "Lady of Heaven." One of the first written hymns is in her honor and dates from 2300 B.C.E. It was her high priestess, Enheduanna, who wrote the hymn, addressed to the Beloved of Heaven who has regained her place in the Sumerian pantheon.

> *Oh my Lady, Beloved of Heaven.... The day is auspicious. The priestess is clothed in beautiful robes, in womanly beauty, as if in the light of the rising moon. The gods have appeared in their rightful places, the doorsill of Heaven cries "Hail!" Praise...to my lady enfolded in beauty. Praise to Inanna. (Women in Praise of the Sacred, Jane Hirshfield, 6-7)*

The priestess was clothed in the light of the rising moon. The moon goddess Inanna, enfolded in beauty, was being feted. The language is beautiful. The words of hymn themselves are sensual and direct, "in womanly beauty." They hint of intimacy with the sacred.

Skipping ahead through the centuries, we stop in the 6th sixth century B.C.E. with Sappho, the Greek lyrical poet born on the island of Lesbos. She devoted her life to composing poems to celebrate beauty, songs of love and longing, performed with the accompaniment of a lyre. Here is an excerpt from one of the remaining fragments of her work. Sappho is encouraging her companion Kika to adorn herself in beauty, to bind her hair with lovely crowns of stems of anise tied together.

> *For the blessed Graces prefer to look on one*
> *who wears flowers*
> *   And turn away from those without a crown.*
> *(Fragments of Sappho, Anne Carson, 157)*

The Graces prefer those who braid their hair with flowers. They disregard those who are not graced with a beautiful crown. In reading these words, we wish to follow suit. Beauty is a gift to be cultivated. We wish to braid our own hair with flowers.

I have already cited the teaching of Socrates in Plato's dialogue "Phaedrus," in my first chapter, how the effect of beauty on the soul leads it to awaken, to grow wings, and the wings to moisten and to swell. Here, I turn to his dialogue, "Symposium," where Socrates relates the words of the philosopher and priestess Diotima, who speaks of the progression of beauty's effect on humankind. Earthly beauty as perceived by the senses transports the soul to celestial beauty. Diotima describes the ascent from earthly beauty to arrive at the ideal form of beauty.

> *The true order is to begin from the beauties of earth and mount upwards for the sake of that other beauty, using these as steps only, and from one [fair form] going on to all fair forms, and from fair forms to fair notions until from fair notions to the notion of absolute beauty....*
> *Man should live in contemplation of beauty. (Symposium, par. 211)*

In Diotima's words, each manifestation of beauty becomes a stepping-stone from earth to heaven, to the essence of beauty.

We turn to Augustine, who honors beauty in his autobiography, *Confessions*, written in 400 C.E. Augustine recounts his search for God and his spiritual awakening that turned him away from a life of debauchery. Following upon his conversion, and later in his life, he asked himself what he loved most in loving God.

> *I asked the earth, I asked the sea and the deeps, among the living animals, the things that creep. I asked the winds that blow, I asked the heavens, the sun, the moon, the stars, and to all things that stand at the doors of my flesh.... My question was the gaze I turned to them. Their answer was their beauty. (Confessions, 202)*

Their answer was their beauty. Nothing more. After so many years of wasted youth and blinded pursuits, it was the earth, the living animals, the heavens that opened his eyes to their creator. How deeply he chides himself for not finding God sooner.

> *Too late came I to love thee! Beauty, ever*
> *ancient, ever new, too late came I to love thee.*
> *(idem, 222)*

His lament resonates in our hearts. Would that we not come too late to celebrate and love beauty.

We move on through the Middle Ages, remembering first Hildegard of Bingen, German Benedictine Abbess, philosopher, healer, musician, mystic of the 12th century, who celebrated the greenness of nature, calling it *viriditas*, the lushness and verdure of the creation, the greening power of God.

And we pause to appreciate St. Francis of Assisi, whose heart was captured by the beauty of the natural world. He composed "The Canticle of the Creatures" in 1225, to praise God for the creatures, the sun, moon, stars, the wind, water, fire, earth.

> *Praised be You, my Lord, with all Your creatures,*
> *especially Sir Brother Sun, who is the day and*
> *through whom You give us light.*

Francis praises God through the beauty of the creation, from Brother Sun who gives us light to Sister Moon and the stars in heaven. From Brother Fire to Sister Mother Earth, "who produces various fruit with colored flowers and herbs." The beauty of the creation—Sun, Moon, Fire, Earth—reflects the beauty of its Creator.

Next we come to the Romantic poets of the early 19th century: Keats, Shelley, Byron, Wordsworth. It was Keats, the passionate lover of beauty in nature, women, and art, who gave us the words, "a thing of beauty is a joy forever." He died so young, at 26 years old, from tuberculosis. As death was closing in upon him, he wrote his most celebrated poems.

Among them is the "Ode to a Grecian Urn," in which he turns to beauty to communicate the truth of human existence.

> *Ah, happy, happy boughs! That cannot shed*
> *Your leaves, nor ever bid the Spring adieu.*

The boughs will stay green and, Keats continues, the melodist will keep piping new songs. And then as old age wastes this generation, the urn alone shall remain. The poet closes with his well-known couplet,

> *"Beauty is truth, truth beauty," - that is all*
> *Ye know on earth, and all ye need to know.*

This deathless piece of beauty, the Grecian urn, with its evergreen boughs will forever remind its beholder that only beauty and truth are eternal. We are finite; beauty and truth are infinite. As we walk through life and search for truth, we find it in beauty.

We arrive now to modern times, when scientific and technical progress have often overshadowed our love of beauty. Humanity in our developed countries is wrapped in the material—the quantifiable. It is as if we wear blinders preventing us from seeing the spiritual—the immeasurable. We are caught up in the frenzy of our everyday lives. We no longer take time to stop and behold the beauty surrounding us. But our poets and mystics continue to remind us where to look, where to cast our eyes.

There is Rainer Maria Rilke, 1875-1926, who writes of beauty as communion with the ineffable. As mentioned in Chapter Two, Rilke corresponded with a young man who wanted to be a poet. In *Letters to a Young Poet,* Rilke gives precious counsel, advising him to commune with nature.

Poetry will follow. As will the belief in some sort of beauty. Nature is our one true teacher.

Almost 20 years later, in his finest work, the *Duino Elegies*, he expands this theme, celebrating the awe-inspiring beauty that opens our hearts and imaginations to our Creator.

> *There remains for us perhaps some tree on the slope, that we might see it again daily.... Several stars presumed you'd be able to feel them. (The First Elegy, 27-28)*

Every day we can bring beauty into our vision: the tree on the slope, the stars waiting for us to see and to feel them. In so doing, our imagination is transported from the creation to the Creator.

Let us listen once again to Thomas Merton, the Trappist monk 1915-1968, whose first introduction to the Christian faith happened in front of a Byzantine icon of Christ's face in a church in Rome. The beauty of the icon overwhelmed him. There were still many steps in his path before becoming a monk and spending the remaining 30 years of his life in a monastery in Kentucky, but Merton had been touched by beauty. The icon opened the door to the spiritual world.

Merton kept journals, he wrote hundreds of letters, he authored over 70 books. As we read his journals, we appreciate his deepening power of attention. His writing sharpens our own sense of beauty. Here is an excerpt where he is seeing beauty in the woods surrounding his hermitage. This seeing transports him to the source of all beauty.

> *April 23 [1964], Sometimes I suddenly see "heavenliness." For instance, in the pure, pure white of the mature dogwood blossoms against the dark evergreens in the cloudy garden.... I*

115

have a sense that this underlying heavenliness
is the real nature of things. (A Vow of Conver-
sation, 44)

Merton is writing here about the art and practice of seeing. The beauty of the pure white dogwood blossom against the dark evergreen revealing the heavenliness of all things. It is the seeing that brings about the union of the visible world and the invisible world.

His last and strongest numinous experience was in front of the mammoth Buddhist statues in Polonnaruwa, Sri Lanka, just days before his untimely death December 8, 1968. His Asian journey came clear. In his words, he was jerked clean of his past life. He experienced a final moment of transcendence. "I don't know when in my life I have ever had such a sense of beauty and spiritual validity running together in one aesthetic illumination." (*The Asian Journal, 235*)

Before concluding this short history of the reverence for beauty over the centuries, I cite one more well-loved poet, author, and priest, John O'Donohue, 1956-2008, especially known for interpreting Celtic spirituality. Like Thomas Merton (interesting to note that both died most unfortunately in their early 50's) he saw beauty as the radiance of the Eternal. In his book *Beauty, the Invisible Embrace,* he wrote that whenever we awaken beauty, we are helping to make God present in the world. Whenever we lift our heads at night to behold the star-studded sky, we are sharing our vision of the divine.

The earth is full of thresholds where beauty awaits our gaze. Here is the poet describing one such threshold:

I was out on Loch Corrib, the largest lake in the
West of Ireland. The lake slept without a ripple.
A gray blue haze enfolded everything.... Then a

harsh flutter as the lake surface split and a huge
cormorant flew from inside the water and struck
up into the air. Its ragged black wings and large
awkward shape were like an eruption from
the underworld.... The strange beauty of the
cormorant was a counterpoint to the dreamlike
delicacy of the lake. (Beauty, The Invisible
Embrace, 11-12)

Here there is not only the beauty of the sleeping lake in the daze of blue; there is also the fearsome beauty of the huge black cormorant erupting from below the surface. Beauty is both the soft blue and the hard black. O'Donohue believed that the presence of the contemplative and the artist is ultimately an invitation to awaken to beauty. "When we beautify our gaze, the grace of hidden beauty becomes our joy and sanctuary."

O'Donohue reminds us that the world is an electro-magnetic field. When we beautify our gaze, we train our eyes to see the flow of different colors in the spectrum. Each plant, each flower, each ripple on the lake, comes alive in the ray of sunlight. We awaken to beauty, and beauty awakens us to the Eternal.

A writing suggestion:

Take a moment to write a journal entry about an experience of beauty. Close your eyes and remember a walk, some tree on a hillside, a sunset, a single star. An encounter with beauty. Describe what you saw, what you felt.

2. Beauty Seen by CG Jung

How does Jung relate to the call of beauty? Let's turn first to *Memories, Dreams, Reflections*. Jung remembers as a young child feeling deep happiness when he was close to a body of water. Once when his mother took him to visit friends who had a castle on Lake Constance, he remembers an unimaginable pleasure.

> *I could not be dragged away from the water. The waves from the steamer washed up on the shore, the sun glistened on the water, and the sand under the water had been curled into little ridges by the waves. The lake stretched away and away in the distance. This expanse of water was an inconceivable pleasure to me, an incomparable splendor. At that time the idea became fixed in my mind that I must live near a lake; without water, I thought, nobody could live at all. (MDR, 22)*

And indeed Jung would build his tower at Bollingen on the shores of the lake of Zurich. As we will read in Chapter Eight, it was here where Jung felt he was in the midst of his true life. "Where I am most deeply myself." (idem, 252)

Much later, as an adult visiting Kenya and Uganda, Jung wrote glowingly about the beauty of the sunrise. Each morning he would take his camp stool and sit under an umbrella acacia just before dawn to watch the sun rise out of darkness. Before him, at the bottom of the little valley, lay a dark strip of jungle. The horizon would become radiantly white.

> *Gradually the swelling light seemed to penetrate into the very structure of the objects which became illuminated from within until at last they shone translucently like bits of colored glass.*

118

> *Everything turned to flaming crystal.... At such*
> *moments I felt as if I were inside a temple. It was*
> *the most sacred hour of the day. I drank in this*
> *glory with insatiable delight, or rather in a time-*
> *less ecstasy. (idem, 298)*

The beauty of the sunrise transported Jung into a moment of timeless bliss. It was the gateway to an experience of transcendence.

It is also in his letters to Emma, his wife, that we discover Jung's attention to the beauty of his surroundings, along with his desire to share it. When we read the letter he wrote to Emma from the Steamer Kaiser Wilhelm der Grosse on his way home from America, his description of the sea takes us back to the attraction of water on Jung as a child, and we appreciate its deep-rooted appeal. It compels Jung to silence.

> *September 22, 1909*
> *One looks out silently, surrendering all self-*
> *importance.... The sea is like music; it has all the*
> *dreams of the soul within itself and sounds them*
> *over. The beauty and grandeur of the sea consists*
> *in our being forced down into the fruitful bottom-*
> *lands of our own psyches, where we confront and*
> *re-create ourselves." (idem, 401-02)*

Throughout his long life, Jung turned to beauty to illuminate his path. As we know, he created the beautiful *Red Book* to contain and honor his visions. He transcribed his journal writings with impressive calligraphy. And he went further and embellished them with stunning paintings. Their striking beauty not only expresses the value Jung gave to each image but also gives witness to the depth of each of Jung's experiences.

*I always knew that these experiences contained
something precious, and therefore I knew of
nothing better than to write them down in a
precious, that is to say costly, book and to paint
the images that emerged through reliving it all
as well as I could. (The Red Book, 360)*

Through painting, the images became precious objects.
Their beauty served to deepen the consciousness of what each
vision revealed. Their contents became intensely alive and
remain so for his readers today. If we look at the painting Jung
did to accompany his chapter "The Gift of Magic," we are almost
physically touched by its beauty. The painting illustrates the
power of the way where the Below and the Above unite. Jung
sees that the power of the way is in the One. "Night sinks blue
and deep from above, earth rises black from below." (idem, 309)

It is through the beauty of his painting that the
numinous quality of his experience shines forth. The
coniunctio, the union, of light and darkness, of above and
below, is made visible. We see the dark rising from the earth
through the roots of the tree up through its branches and the
blue of night descending. And the setting sun shines in a
luminous mandala. Its beauty lifts our spirit, and we touch the
eternal. In the center of the mandala, there is the very inner
circle, full of light, filled with cuneiform figures representing
eternity. Then a gorgeous burst of light reaches outward with
16 sun rays to five concentric circles, each circle a bit dimmer,
as the light spreads through the creation. And high up in the
middle of the branches lingers the distant moon.

Jung, in drawing this superb painting, has brought the
two worlds together. We see in the very center of the mandala
the Self radiating light throughout the creation. It is this
painting that I keep in view in my study, opening myself to
its beauty. Opening myself to the eternal.

Night Sinks Blue, C.G. Jung
Image 131, The Red Book

3. Beauty Seen by Simone Weil

This numinous quality in seeing beauty is echoed in the writings of Simone Weil, the French philosopher, mystic, and political activist, a contemporary of Jung. Wanting to share the conditions of those who suffered the most, the workers in France before World War II, and the wounded in London during the war, she let herself die of malnutrition. Weil saw beauty as the most natural portal to the realm of the transcendent. In her book, *Waiting for God*, she writes, that there remains rooted in the heart of every human an appreciation of beauty. The soul has a natural inclination to love beauty. "The love of beauty proceeds from God dwelling in our souls and goes out to God present in the universe." (*Waiting for God,* 165) As we reach out to beauty in nature—in the splendor of the heavens, the sea, and the mountains—and in true marriage and love, where shines however dimly a reflection of heavenly splendor, we reach out to universal beauty.

To explain this transcendent quality of beauty, Weil introduces the metaphor of the labyrinth. The beauty we see leads us into the labyrinth where the eternal awaits us in the center.

> *The beauty of the world is the mouth of a labyrinth. The unwary individual who on entering takes a few steps, walks on without knowing anything.... If he goes on walking, it is absolutely certain that he will finally arrive at the center of the labyrinth. And there God is waiting to eat him. Later he will go out again, but he will be changed. He will have become different. Afterward he will stay near the entrance so that he can gently push all those who come near into the opening." (idem, 163)*

Weil illustrates this with the story of Cora, known better as Persephone, who admiring the fresh beauty of the narcissus, smelling its scent, reached out her hand and was caught by Hades the ruler of the Underworld. We read in the myth,

> *In his chariot drawn by coal-black steeds he rose*
> *up through a chasm in the earth, and grasping*
> *the maiden by the wrist set her beside him. He*
> *bore her away weeping, down to the underworld.*
> *(Edith Hamilton, Mythology, 50)*

Beauty was the trap that enticed Persephone. Hardly had she stopped to appreciate the flowering narcissus than she fell into the hands of the living God. I pause here, thinking how extraordinary is this retelling of the myth of Persephone. So often we dwell on her mother Demeter's crying out for her daughter, who has disappeared from face of the earth, and we overlook how it happened. It was beauty that permitted Hades to kidnap her. We can imagine ourselves being taken by a sight of exquisite beauty and then carried away to the under-world, to the divine.

I return to the labyrinth that Weil has evoked. The labyrinth is one of the most ancient symbols of humanity, dating back to 2500 B.C.E. and older. From petroglyphs in Goa, courtyards in ancient Egypt, carved rocks in Greece, palaces in Crete (Knossos), throughout the centuries to the Gothic Cathedrals of Chartres, Reims, Amiens, the labyrinth continues to express a universal, archetypal longing for the sacred. Here is a representation of the pavement labyrinth at Chartres, 1220 C.E., where it filled the center of the nave, inviting worshippers to walk its path to God at the center.

Labyrinth at Chartres Cathedral

It was also a representation of the pilgrimage to Jerusalem. The worshippers who could not make the actual pilgrimage were able to make it by following the serpentine path of the labyrinth. We see here an archetypal symbol of the psyche representing the path of individuation. Jung described the labyrinth as "a primordial image which one encounters in psychology mostly in the form of the fantasy of a descent to the underworld." (Letter to Karl Kerenyi, March 10, 1941). We think of Jung's own descent related in *The Red Book*. We think also of our own pilgrimage through life, following the path of individuation.

At the Chartres Cathedral, the labyrinth is most often covered with chairs for the liturgies. However at the Grace Cathedral in San Francisco, it is outside, beautifully set in stone. I was able to walk it the morning it was to be inaugurated. People were busy making certain everything was ready. I was alone, in my own world. When I reached the center, the bells and recording of Amazing Grace started to play. A moment of transcendence.

When we walk the labyrinth today, we may think of three movements in our pilgrimage:

—Releasing, as we enter, we let go of the details of our life, we follow a winding path into the unconscious always deeper to the center.

—Receiving, as we rest in the center, we receive whatever gift is there, a gift from God, Allah, the Tao, the awareness of the Self.

—Returning, as we leave to return to the outside world, we carry with us what we have received as healing energy, as love.

We experience the three movements as a path to individuation, a path to the center. And when we return to the outside world, Weil instructs us to stay near the entrance in order to encourage others to enter. To encourage others to respond to the call of beauty. We cannot horde the gifts of the labyrinth. They are there to be shared. Indeed, this is what Jung did in creating *The Red Book*. Jung wanted to give his visions the beautiful expression that they deserved. And it is what Sonu Shamdasani, the editor and translator, and all those involved in its publication, did in making *The Red Book*, this gift of the labyrinth, available to all of us.

We, too, may follow our image into the labyrinth, as Persephone followed her narcissus into the underworld. Let our image lead us into this winding path to the center.

125

A visualizing suggestion:

If you wish, I suggest you imagine following your image into the labyrinth pictured above. Perhaps follow the path with your pencil lightly. When in the center, rest and receive. When ready to leave, return to the entrance.

4. Beauty Celebrated by a few Contemporary Writers

In our own individual lives, how do we respond to the call of beauty? How do we practice this art of seeing? I evoke the examples of two contemporary authors who each celebrated beauty in the world around them.

Terry Tempest Williams

First, Terry Tempest Williams, whom I introduced in Chapter Two, Pursuing Your Images. Here I turn to her book *Finding Beauty in a Broken World,* which she wrote in response to the terror and destruction of 9/11. She was at a loss as to how to continue to create, how to continue her work as a writer. "The peace in our own hearts is shattered, how to pick up the pieces?"

Williams accepts the invitation to accompany as a scribe the visionary artist Lily Yeh to Rwanda, where with other barefoot artists they will create a genocide memorial honoring the 800,000 Tutsis massacred in 100 days in 1994. Williams turns to art to witness how beauty emerges out of brokenness.

She gathers the stories of death and resilience as she helps the survivors gather the rubble of war. Together with the artists day by day, they build a mosaic of beauty over the buried bones. The village is rebirthing through art.

> *This I have witnessed: There is a village in Rwanda that is in the process of painting itself alive, breathing life back into its community through color and the joyful emancipatory gesture of creating beauty. (Finding Beauty in a Broken World, 336)*

In helping to build this memorial, Williams illustrates the healing power of beauty. There was a coming together of families, of artists, of survivors. There is within all humanity, the call to create beauty.

> *Mosaic celebrates brokenness and the beauty of being brought together....*
>   *The gift of an attentive life is the ability to find our way toward a unity built on empathy. Empathy becomes the path that leads us from the margins to the center of concern. (idem, 385)*

A path from the margins to the center. Williams is showing us the way. A path designed through empathy toward the unity of humankind. We are back to the mandalas that Jung drew. All paths were leading to the center. And to Weil's labyrinth. Terry Tempest Williams was caught by beauty. She followed it to the center in helping to create the mosaic memorial in Rwanda and then returned to the circumference in being the scribe and giving us her book.

Marion Woodman

Another writer who celebrated beauty is Marion Woodman, a much appreciated voice in feminine development and a Jungian analyst. In her book *Bone, Dying into Life,* she recounts in journal form the story of her illness (uterine cancer), her healing process, her journey to transforming herself. From research, Woodman writes that there is no exact explanation for the "miracle of healing." She also learned that the images that feed us affect the white blood cells that strengthen the immune system. This fact uplifts her spirit and sustains her throughout the journal writing. She will pay attention to the images of beauty around her.

Here is a passage written the day of her return home after her major surgery.

> *November 22, 1993*
> *Put flowers in every room. Take delight every morning in giving them fresh water, cutting their stems, seeing their faces—especially now the lilies with their sexy stamens and pistils—the whole of the life process involved. In their gradual opening, singing their glorias, they are magnifying God. And then the inevitable transparency in their petals as they change color. Then their silent letting go.... The hour I spend with them every morning is healing for me. (Bone, 23)*

Every morning Woodman feeds her flowers and treats herself to their beauty. And every morning they feed her and bring healing. She sees in them the whole of life's cycle, from their gradual opening to their letting go. She treasures them with her words.

Near the end of her journal, she writes about going with her husband, Ross, to see the wild swans making their way to Grand Bend. This, too, is part of her healing, seeing the swans take flight.

March 15, 1995
What glory! As they rise from the cornfields to fly
to the water they are right over our heads. We can
see the lace of their wings, pristine white, and
hear their sad call. Such elegance—every one in
perfect formation position, flying full stretched....
As the line of swans fly into the sunset, they are
white crests on elongated ocean waves, their
wings moving in slow rhythm like the everlasting
motion of the waters. (idem, 235-236)

In comparing the motion of their wings to the ever-lasting motion of water, Woodman reminds us of Jung's attraction to water, to its beauty and its movement. The everlasting motion of water is a lure. Beauty is a lure. We are captivated by the flight of wild geese. We are lifted out of ourselves, into the invisible world, where body and spirit are one. This was the healing for Marion Woodman.

Susan Tiberghien

Before closing this chapter, I share here how I practice this art of seeing. Almost daily I turn my attention to an image of beauty: the sunlight on the lake, the Japanese maple, the forsythia in early spring, the cluster of birds at the feeder. And inside my home: the nautilus shell on my desk, the freshly cut flowers, a peony in a pewter vase on my table. I look at the deep pink petals, I close my eyes and imagine entering them, gently brushing each one aside to reach the center. I pause and find rest in the center, there where Jung places the Self, his God-image. And I write about it in my journal.

In my most recent book, *Side by Side*, a memoir of our long marriage, I start each chapter with a journal entry about an image of nature that has caught my attention. The image—a maple leaf, sunflowers, evergreen ivy, an acorn, a mountain lake—becomes a lure leading me deeper in my reflections and writing. I continue to write page after page as I follow the object into the labyrinth of our relationship. Here is an excerpt from the journal entry about the evergreen ivy that covers the wall outside our home.

> *Geneva, October 20*
> *When Pierre and I went out this morning, I looked at the ivy on the wall by our front door. The leaves glistened in the sunlight. I focused on just a few leaves, seeing each single leaf shining, reaching upward with its little buds. Each leaf a whole world in itself.*
>
> *As I write, I see the ivy anew in my imagination.... I think of Basho who wrote that poetry arises when we plunge deep enough into what we are looking at "to see something like a hidden light glimmering there." This is what I want to do with the images that I write about. To plunge into them. And see a light glimmering....*
>
> *Nature is becoming my church. The changing colors, my liturgy.... It is my Sunday reading. I could make it my daily reading. (Side by Side, 130-131)*

I write about the beauty of each single leaf shining in the early morning sunlight. Each leaf a mystery, a whole world in itself. And yes, I want to plunge into it. To follow it to the center, to a glimmering light. I write about the experience in my journal. And I take a photo of my evergreen ivy with its white buds waiting to flower in winter. I think of

The Way of Evergreen Ivy

The Red Book, of Jung counseling Christina Morgan to keep a journal, telling her, telling all of us, that the journal will be our cathedral, the place of our soul.

To look at an object of nature and awaken to its beauty. Then to write about it in a journal entry. It is now your turn to return to your image and write about it. To see beauty with your words. To let beauty show the way to the Infinite.

A writing suggestion:

Return to your image. Maybe close your eyes and hold on to it. See it. Then write a few words to describe the experience and to celebrate beauty.

In conclusion, when we respond to beauty this way, we are honoring and protecting not only the beauty in our lives and our surroundings, but also the beauty in the entire creation. Our universe is a whole. What we touch affects the totality. In painting his vision of the union of Below and Above—the beauty of night sinking blue and earth rising black—Jung has touched millions of souls. And we today, when we share beauty's radiance with our words, we are sharing its radiance with the world around us.

Chapter Six

Practicing Alchemy: From Darkness to Light

"Darkness gives birth to light...what is unconscious
becomes conscious."
C.G. Jung

"What the written word could express only imperfectly,
the alchemist compressed into his images."
C.G. Jung

Why was Jung so moved upon reading *The Secret of the Golden Flower*, so deeply moved that he put aside *The Red Book* and turned his attention to furthering his study of alchemy? And why today are we interested in alchemy? We will look first at its meaning and at how it has been practiced through the centuries. With this understanding, we will better appreciate how Jung was able to discover the parallels between the alchemical procedures and his analytical psychology. Indeed, how he saw the practice of alchemy as an exploration of the self.

We will then study the steps of alchemy—*nigredo, albedo, rubedo*—and see how they correspond to the steps of individuation. How they can help us deepen our own exploration of self. We will read excerpts from *The Red Book* and *Memories, Dreams, Reflections.* And lastly we will look at the work of several contemporary authors, including

Margaret Atwood, Paolo Coelho, Joseph Brodsky, with examples of how they write from darkness to light. We will become alchemists ourselves.

1. Introduction and History of Alchemy

Before looking at alchemy and the past, let us look at the intensely dark, difficult time we live in: wars, terrorism, mass immigration, famine, climate change. We are at a loss how to intervene. It is extremely difficult to not feel power-less. Yet we have stories throughout the centuries of incredibly brave souls who confronted the darkness. There is St. John of the Cross, imprisoned in a dungeon in Toledo, when he wrote *Dark Night of the Soul*. There is Dante, writing in *The Divine Comedy*, "Midway upon the journey of our life, I found that I was in a dusky wood." There is Jung himself and his willed descent into the unconscious where for 16 years he searched for his way. Etty Hillesum, who confronted her approaching death at Auschwitz, with the words, "We have only one moral duty, to reclaim the peace within us and to radiate it around us." And Martin Luther King, who in the midst of racial violence and hatred, shortly before his assassination, wrote, "The arc of the moral universe is long, but it always bends toward justice."

How do we find the courage to confront darkness? To reclaim those areas of peace? Alchemy will show us the way. Let us remember Jung's early dream, when in the night he was making slow headway against a mighty wind. He had his hands cupped around a tiny light. Everything depended on his keeping that little light alive. Each of us carries a light, lit by a divine spark within us. All our creation myths speak to this: the fiery sparks, the seeds of light, the Gnostic *scintillae*, the shards in the Zohar. To uncover these sparks, to reclaim the peace within us, we will learn from the alchemists.

This ancient practice sought to transform nonprecious metals, lead and copper, into precious metals, silver and gold. It was a physical discipline. As alchemists realized that the transformation of metals could serve as a metaphor for the transformation of human nature, it became a spiritual discipline. Not only were the alchemists looking to transform matter, they were looking to transform themselves. To find the silver and gold within.

The word comes from the Greek *chemeia,* derived from *Khem*, an ancient name for Egypt, and the Arabic definite article *al.* Its roots are hence Greek, Egyptian, and Arabic. The earliest existing alchemical texts in the Western world are papyri in Greek that describe this mysterious art, which originated in Egypt. Marie-Louise von Franz, a colleague of Jung, in her book *Alchemy, An Introduction to the Symbolism and the Psychology*, defines alchemy as a natural science that attempts to understand the mystery of nature. Let us stay with this definition.

We can depict this mystery in three different ways.

—From earliest times, alchemy has been a chemical practice to find the gold in base metals, to find the Philosopher's Stone.

—Progressively, it became a spiritual practice to find the sparks of the Creator within the creation, to find the world soul, *anima mundi.*

—And more recently in psychological terms, it is understood as a psychological practice to find the self, the archetype of wholeness.

The goal is the same: to unveil the mystery of nature.

From Egypt, we have one of the oldest known Western alchemical texts, "The Prophetess Isis to Her Son," dating back to the first century C.E. During the Roman Empire, Isis was renowned as an alchemist. The text relates a much older legend. Marie-Louise von Franz gives her account of the legend in her book *Alchemy*. When one of the angels wanted to make love to Isis, she asked him first for the alchemical secret of making gold, the elixir of life. The angel said that this was beyond his knowledge and sent her a greater angel. The greater angel also wanted to make love to Isis. He did give her the secret, instructing her to tell no one except her son. It is not known if they made love.

Von Franz recounts the antique recipe for the elixir of alchemy. It begins "Take quicksilver, fix it in lumps of earth or sulfur and retain it, this is fixation through heat; then take one part lead, two parts white stone, mix and reduce...." (*Alchemy*, 50). The recipe continues for paragraphs, growing more and more complex and arcane. We see here that alchemy was born through the resistance of Isis to the angel. As von Franz writes, "Isis founded alchemy; she did something with it, whereas the angel just kept it to himself." (idem, 63)

From this ancient legend in Egypt, we move to the teachings and writings of Aristotle, fourth century B.C.E. in Greece. He believed that all things tend toward perfection. Since gold is the most perfect metal, he thought it was reasonable to believe that nature created it out of other metals hidden deep within the earth. Echoing the recipe from the Prophetess Isis, Aristotle gave instructions to whiten the earth, sublime it with fire, until the Spirit within was released. He defined the whitened earth as "quintessence," the fifth element to place next to fire, air, water, earth.

If we turn to the other side of the world, we have the text *The Secret of the Golden Flower,* attributed to Lü Yen of the ninth century C.E., who himself traced back the origin of this secret lore to Lao Tsu and the *Tao Te Ching*. It is this text that so impressed Jung when Richard Wilhelm, the German sinologist and missionary from China, sent it to him asking if he would write a commentary. The text is an amalgam of ancient Taoist and Buddhist ideas, using alchemical symbols to describe the transformation of the human soul. By joining the personal spirit and soul to the transpersonal spirit and soul, the golden flower is formed. The golden flower is a symbol for true consciousness, for the awareness of the Higher Self.

There is an 18th-century engraving that pictures a pair of alchemists at work, producing precisely the golden flower. The engraving is from *Mutus liber, Mute Book,* first published in 1677. Jung had a copy of the first edition and used it to illustrate his work, *Psychology and Alchemy*. I include it here to show the flower in both the third and fourth drawings.

We note that the alchemists are pictured as two, male and female, that there is a *coniunctio* here, a coming together, male and female. They are inserting the base metals into the alembic to be fired in the furnace. After the firing and distillation, the golden flower is formed. In the fourth drawing the female alchemist is carefully removing the golden flower. Together they will start once again the process.

Alchemists at Work, 18th century manuscript

To continue our review of the history of alchemy, we return to Greece, to Zosimos of Panopolis, a fourth-century C.E. alchemist and mystic who wrote one of the earliest books on alchemy, *Concerning the True Book of Sophe, the Egyptian.* He defined alchemy as embodying and disembodying, as freeing the spirits from the body and then bonding them back together with the body. The transformation of lead and copper into silver and gold had always to mirror an inner process of purification and redemption. He imagined the alchemical vessel as a baptismal font for the spiritual transformation, and the vapors of mercury and sulfur as the purifying waters of baptism. From his many dreams and visions, alchemy became much more a religious experience than a protoscience. Jung in *Memories, Dreams, Reflections,* refers to Zosimos's visions, comparing them to the text of the Mass in Catholic liturgy.

We turn now to medieval Islam and the Arabian alchemist, of the 10th century, Ibn Umail, also known as Senior Zadith or just Senior. As his predecessors, Senior saw alchemy as a spiritual operation. In his text, *De Chemia*, there is a drawing of a winged bird (soul) and wingless bird (*prima materia*) holding on to each other. The inscription reads, "The wingless bird prevents the winged bird from flying away, while the winged bird wants to raise the wingless bird." (M.L. von Franz, *Alchemy,* 114) Ibn Umail felt that the allegorical meaning of alchemy was to produce the winged bird. But to do so the wingless bird must first be unearthed and freed. We see here the interconnection between the lower and the upper worlds, between the *prima materia* and the soul.

In the 16th century in Europe, there were the Swiss physician and alchemist Paracelsus and his disciple Gerhard Dorn, the first Western alchemist to recognize that the Philosopher's Stone was hidden in the individual and that the goal could be reached by reflection and meditation. Dorn was one of Jung's most frequently cited alchemists. He elaborated three steps in the alchemical process:

—First separate the soul from the body and unite it with the spirit.

—Then reunite the soul and spirit with the body which has been cleansed, thereby producing the Philosopher's Stone.

—And finally unite the now joined soul, spirit, body with the original *unus mundus*, the world in which all is one, the unitary world beyond the microcosm and macrocosm.

From these steps, we see the ancient formula, *solve et coagula*, to dissolve and coagulate. To transform—be it metals to gold, or human nature to transcendence—there is first the breaking down of elements and then the coming together. And we remember the "disembodying and embodying" of the Greek alchemist Zosimos. To draw the spirits from the bodies and then bond the cleansed spirits back within the bodies. *Solve et coagula*. Separate and join together.

Entering the Age of Reason, alchemy was mistrusted and considered to be the pursuit of magic. The scientific revolution with Copernicus and Galileo, followed by the Age of Reflection with Descartes and John Locke in the 17th century, established reason as the primary source of authority. The scientific method was the rule. Who could believe that base metals could be turned into gold? It was all superstition.

So it remained until the last century and C.G. Jung. With years of study of alchemical texts, Jung was able to document in *Psychology and Alchemy*, 1944, his realization that the different alchemical procedures represented symbolically the exploration of the unconscious and hence the individuation process. The Philosopher's Stone, the goal of the alchemical opus, was a symbol of the Self.

The door was now opened to the proper appreciation of the art of alchemy. Whether it be in chemical, spiritual, or psychological terms, the practice of alchemy aspired to the union of matter and spirit in its quest for the transcendent.

Let us pause here to consider what alchemy might mean for us. An attempt through chemistry to turn lead into gold? Or a spiritual practice to find the gold within? Or do we view it more as a psychological practice to help us find meaning in our lives?

A writing suggestion:

Take a few minutes to describe how you see alchemy today. What does the word summon up for you? What image comes to your mind? Write a few lines.

2. Jung's Long Study of Alchemy

We turn now to Jung's long study of alchemy, going back to the year 1928, when Jung received the Chinese alchemical text *The Secret of the Golden Flower,* sent to him by his friend, the eminent German Sinologist Richard Wilhelm, who requested a commentary. Upon reading, the text brought to Jung the unforeseen confirmation of what he had uncovered in his confrontation with the unconscious, of his 16 years of reflection contained in *The Red Book* and in the psychic development of his patients.

Jung had earlier just finished his next-to-last painting in *The Red Book.* It was a mandala with a golden castle in the middle. Jung wrote in his autobiography, "When it was finished, I asked myself, 'Why is this so Chinese?' I was impressed by the form and choice of colours, which seemed to me Chinese." (*MDR,* 222) It was a strange coincidence that shortly afterward Wilhelm sent him the text of *The Secret of the Golden Flower*. As he studied the Chinese text, Jung saw in his painting, a representation of what he was reading; he saw the golden flower and its path to transcendence. In remembrance of this synchronicity, Jung wrote underneath the painting, "In 1928 when I was painting this picture, showing the golden, well-fortified castle, Richard Wilhelm sent me the thousand year old Chinese text on the yellow castle, the germ of the immortal body." (*MDR*, 223) For Jung, this was an early example of synchronicity, bridging over the seeming disunion between the physical world and the psychic. (Murray Stein, *Jung's Map of the Soul,* p.209)

It was the text of *The Secret of the Golden Flower* that broke through Jung's isolation and led him to delving more deeply into the study of alchemy. He had grown familiar with alchemical texts from 1920 onward, and now he was no longer alone. He could listen to these ancient alchemists, committed to the discovery of the meaning of creation. As Shamdasani points out in his introduction to *The Red Book*, Jung's understanding of alchemy was based on his thesis that the symbolism in the alchemists' texts corresponded to that of the individuation process with which he and his patients were engaged.

In his Commentary to *The Secret of the Golden Flower*, he asked himself what the authors of this work did to achieve such deep inner wisdom. "As far as I could see they did nothing, *wu wei* [action through non-action] but let things happen." (93) Jung continued, making reference to Meister Eckhart and the art of letting go of oneself, which "became for me the key opening the door to the way." (ibid.) In listening to these ancient alchemists, Jung learned how they liberated themselves from the control of their consciousness by following the same alchemical methods they used to transform matter.

This understanding is foreshadowed in Jung's encounters with Philemon, the Gnostic and the Alchemist, recorded in *The Red Book*. Jung was growing aware of the vital thread linking his psychology back to alchemy and still further back to Gnosticism. Here is part of the dialogue between Jung and Philemon, the Alchemist, in the section titled "The Magician." Jung had traveled to a far country in search of a great magician of whose reputation he had heard tell. After a long search, he finds the house, fronted by tulips, where the magician Philemon lives with his wife, Baucis.

We remember the myth in Ovid's *Metamorphoses* of Philemon and Baucis, the couple who received the disguised guides and welcomed them to their humble home. In the myth, Ovid gives Baucis a central role. It is she who kills their last goose to give the Gods a worthy meal. And it is their relationship and human love which the Gods celebrate by saving them from the flood and giving them whatever wish they desire. However, when, in *The Red Book*, Jung describes his encounter with the magician, he addresses only Philemon. Baucis stays in the background, she is only Philemon's other half. Jung will learn from Philemon. With time he will learn from Baucis, from his feminine side.

Here is the encounter.

I stand at the garden gate. "Philemon, old magician, how are you?"
P: "I am well, stranger," he says, "but what are you doing here?"
I: "People tell me that you understand the black art. Will you tell me about it?"....
P: "Well, all you will do is laugh.... Why should I tell you anything? It would be better if

> *everything were buried with me. It will never be*
> *lost to humanity, since magic is reborn with each*
> *and every one of us."*
> *I: "What do you mean? Do you believe that*
> *magic is really inborn in man?"*
> *P: "If I could, I would say, yes, of course, it is.*
> *But you will find this laughable,"*
> *(The Red Book, 312)*

The conversation continues, and Jung listens until he is quite dizzy from trying to understand and must leave the garden. In the commentary that follows, he writes:

> *It is an error to believe that there are magical*
> *practices that one can learn.... Magic is a way*
> *of living. If one has done one's best to steer the*
> *chariot, and one then notices that a greater other*
> *is actually steering it, then magical operation*
> *takes place." (idem, 314)*

Jung continues to reflect, the commentary is long. He asks himself if he really left Philemon unsatisfied. No, he left him really satisfied. Satisfied because Philemon's words left him to himself.

> *You are wise, Oh Philemon, but you do not give.*
> *You want your garden to bloom and for every-*
> *thing to grow from within itself. (idem, 316)*

So it was that Jung recognized that Philemon was a magician, that in serving the Gods who visited him, he united the Above and the Below.

For over 10 years Jung deciphered all the alchemical writings he could find, filling eight copybooks with an index for each volume and discovering parallels with his own psychological theories. To find his way about in the labyrinth of alchemical thought processes, he made a lexicon of the strange expressions, the key words and phrases. He soon realized that the experiences of the alchemists were in a sense his experiences, their world was his world.

> *This was a momentous discovery. I had stumbled upon the historical counterpart of my psychology of the unconscious. The possibility of a comparison with alchemy, and the uninterrupted chain back to Gnosticism, gave substance to my psychology. When I pored over the old texts, everything fell into place: the fantasy images, the empirical material I had gathered in my practice, and the conclusions I had drawn from it. (MDR, 231)*

Alchemy formed the bridge on the one hand into the past, to Gnosticism, and on the other into the future, to the modern psychology of the unconscious. The images and symbols in the alchemical manuscripts could be traced back to early Gnostic texts—Jung's first love among esoteric systems—and traced forward to the images and symbols in the dreams of his patients. Alchemy provided the suite to Gnosticism, both systems based on a symbolic approach to understanding the mysteries of life, and confirmed Jung in his belief that we have to turn back to those periods in human history when the formation of images and symbols still went on unimpeded.

> *If one accepts the symbol, it is as if a door opens leading into a new room whose existence one previously did not know.... Salvation is a long road that leads through many gates. These gates are symbols. Each new gate is at first invisible. (The Red Book, 311)*

Jung understood that the three stages of alchemy—*nigredo, albedo, rubedo*—were symbolic representations of the exploration of the unconscious and the development of the self. Each stage was, as it were, a gate to the next.

First there is *nigredo*. In chemical terms, this is the blackening in the furnace, the firing and melting out of impurities. In spiritual terms, it is the separating of the soul from the body so that it can unite with the spirit. For Jung, in psychological terms, it is the descending into the unknown, the ego discovering its shadow in the unconscious, "the hidden, repressed, for the most part inferior personality...but also displaying normal instincts, realistic insights, creative impulses." (*Aion*, 266) It is indeed what Jung experienced from 1913 onward.

The second stage is named *albedo*. In chemical terms, this is the whitening, the washing away of impurities, the constant distilling, the refining process. In spiritual terms, it is the reuniting the soul and spirit with the body which has been washed. For Jung, in psychological terms, it is bringing the shadow to the light, uniting the conscious and the unconscious, the beginning emergence of the self. It is opening "so as to midwife the God." (*The Red Book*, 330)

The third stage is *rubedo*. In chemical terms, this is the reddening, the polishing, the crystallization into the golden flower, the creation of the Philosopher's Stone. In spiritual terms, it is the uniting of the human being—now soul, spirit, body—with the divine. And in psychological aspect, it is the new consciousness, the manifestation of the Self, the God image.

Jung did a stunning painting of the Philosopher's Stone to illustrate a *rubedo* moment in the middle of his journey when he felt affirmed after killing his imagined dragon and ready to listen to the voice of the depths.

The Philosopher's Stone, C.G. Jung
Image 121, The Red Book

He wrote in *The Red Book*:

I feel the things that were and that will be.
Behind the ordinary the eternal abyss yawns.
The earth gives me back what it hid. (idem, 305)

The inscription reads, "This stone, set so beautifully, is certainly the Lapis Philosophorum. It expands into space through four distinct qualities, namely breadth, height, depth, and time. It is hence invisible and you can pass through it without noticing it. The four streams of Aquarius flow from the stone." (ibid, footnote 229)

Jung referred later in his work to this alchemical representation of a circle quadrated by four rivers and commented often on the four rivers of paradise. In giving us this painting, Jung has given us a beautiful symbolic manifestation of the Self. As we look at it, a ray of light enters the unknown within us. Our eyes are drawn to the center, then outward with the four rivers. And then back to the center. As we do this, our own consciousness deepens. This is the third stage of alchemy, *rubedo*.

Seen in this light, *The Red Book* becomes a symbolic alchemical experience. With each vision, each encounter, Jung wrestled with the unknown. He faced the darkness, looked for light, and continued his journey, encountering one figure of his imagination after another.

As I worked with my fantasies, I became aware
that the unconscious undergoes or produces
change. Only after I had familiarized myself with
alchemy did I realize that the unconscious is a
process and that the psyche is transformed or
developed by the relationship of the ego to the
contents of the unconscious. (MDR, 235)

As Shamdasani writes in *C.G. Jung, A Biography in Books,* the study of alchemy presented Jung with a mode to present his researches in an allegorical manner. "In an encrypted manner, images and conceptions from *Liber Novus* surfaced, contextualized and amplified." (*C.G. Jung,* 202). Throughout his work, Jung was depicting symbolically the fruit of the individuation process: the Self, which he saw as the Philosopher's Stone.

We have all experienced descents into darkness, into the unknown. Do you remember one? Without them, there is no depth in our daily lives. This is part of wholeness: recognizing our shadow.

A writing suggestion:

Describe an experience where you descended into darkness either willfully or unknowingly. A few lines, to describe your encounter with the *nigredo* stage of alchemy.

3. Writing from Darkness to Light

Our chapter takes us now to consider how the practice of alchemy shows us a way to write from darkness to light. Enlightenment can come from the dark place, but only if we direct the ray of consciousness upon it. If we warm it by our conscious attention. Authors become alchemists as they write from darkness to light, as they go into the dark, into the unknown, and bring out what they encounter into the light, into the known. It is a perilous journey. We think again of St. John of the Cross, Dante, Jung himself, Etty Hillesum, Martin Luther King. Let us look more at length at the writings of a few contemporary authors who consciously describe the experience.

Margaret Atwood

Margaret Atwood, in her book *Negotiating with the Dead, A Writer on Writing*, speaks of darkness as the home of all our stories. Wealth of every kind, she writes, flows from the invisible world to the visible one. She cites Rilke in his *Sonnets to Orpheus* who makes this underworld journey a precondition of being a poet. "You have to have been among the shades, / tuning your lyre there too, / if you want vision enough to know / how to make lasting praise." Atwood points out that Virgil was not the first to visit the Other World. And she turns to Gilgamesh.

Gilgamesh, the giant from the East whom Jung met on top of the mountain in *The Red Book*. Gilgamesh the semi-mythic Sumerian King who, in mourning the death of his soul mate Enkidu, goes down to the underworld to bring him back to life and to search for the secret of immortality. Atwood used his journey to the underworld as an example.

I was holding forth about this [Gilgamesh's journey] at a dinner for a bunch of writers. "Gilgamesh was the first writer," I said. "He wants the secret of life and death, he goes through hell, he comes back but he hasn't got immortality, all he's got is two stories—the one about his trip, and the other, extra one about the flood. Then he's really, really tired, and then he writes the whole thing down on a stone."

"Yeah, that's what it is," said the writers. "You go, you get the story, you're whacked out, you come back and write it all down on a stone.

"Go where?" I said.

"To where the story is," they said.

Where is the story? The story is in the dark. That is why inspiration is thought of as coming in flashes. Going into a narrative is a dark road. You can't see your way ahead.... The well of inspiration is a hole that leads downwards. (Negotiating with the Dead, 176)

Atwood shows us the way. Go into the dark. Our stories are there. Our source of inspiration is there. We enter the unknown, *nigredo*, to find the story. Then we distill it, *albedo*. And finally we write it, *rubedo*.

Paulo Coelho

I turn to the example of Paulo Coelho, who in his remarkable fable, *The Alchemist,* recounts the story of an Andalusian shepherd boy, Santiago. One night asleep under a sycamore tree near an abandoned church, he dreamed of a treasure of gold buried near the Egyptian pyramids. He sells his flock of sheep and sets out into the unknown. Very soon his money is stolen, and he finds himself penniless in a strange country, *nigredo*. He manages to earn enough money to continue his dream and follows a caravan deep into the desert, where he is confronted by a black-garbed stranger on a white horse, the alchemist. The alchemist teaches Santiago to listen to his heart. From *nigredo* to *albedo*, Santiago is learning how to become an alchemist. Here is how he speaks to the wind to ask for its help as he pursues his dream.

> *"Help me," the boy said....*
> *"Who taught you to speak the language of the desert and the wind?"*
> *"My heart," the boy answered....*
> *"You can't be the wind," the wind said. "We're two very different things."*
> *"That's not true. I learned the alchemist's secrets in my travels. I have inside me the winds,*

the deserts, the stars, and everything created in
the universe. We were all made by the same hand
and we have the same soul. (The Alchemist, 154)

Santiago continues his journey to the very foot of the pyramids. As he is digging to find the treasure, thieves come along, beat him, and take all that he has. One of the thieves reveals to Santiago his own dream that there is gold buried near an abandoned church. Santiago realizes that his treasure is back in Andalusia, where he first dreamed of it. He returns and finds his treasure under the sycamore tree by the abandoned church. *Rubedo.* Coelho has taken not only Santiago on an alchemical voyage, but also the reader.

Joseph Brodsky

Let us look now at the poet and nonfiction writer Joseph Brodsky, who also weaves the stages of alchemy into his writing. Born in 1940 in Leningrad, renamed St. Petersburg, he went into involuntary exile in 1972, settling in the United States. Awarded the Nobel Prize for his poetry, he published a collection of short prose pieces about Venice, titled *Watermark*, recounting his innumerable visits to this magical city.

Here is how he describes the sudden apparition of a ray of light in deep darkness, as he travels with his companion along the Grand Canal in Venice.

The boat's slow progress through the night was
like the passage of a coherent thought through
the sub-conscious. On both sides, knee-deep in
pitch-black water, stood the enormous carved
chests of dark palazzi filled with unfathomable
treasures—most likely gold, judging from the

*low-intensity yellow electric glow emerging now
and then from cracks in the shutters. The overall
feeling was mythological. (Watermark, 13)*

Brodsky describes the experience as following a thought through the unconscious. With his companion, he continues his approach to the landing. Soon they will arrive. There was a hush. The passengers around them, whose number is responsible for their proximity, were immobile and subdued in their occasional remarks.

*Then the sky was momentarily obscured by the
huge marble parenthesis of a bridge, and suddenly
everything was flooded with light. (idem, 14)*

Light! The boat's progress can be seen as an alchemical voyage. First the slow progress in the night, *nigredo*. On both sides, knee-deep in pitch-black water, there are chests of unfathomable treasures, emitting an electric glow through the cracks, *albedo*. And just after passing under a bridge, suddenly there is light, *rubedo*. The passage of a vaporetto in the night, the passage of a thought in the unconscious. In a few paragraphs, Brodsky has moved from darkness to light.

Susan Tiberghien

Before closing this chapter, I give an example from my own writing, from my book *Circling to the Center*. In writing once about a small cinquefoil, the yellow wildflower with five petals, I was taken back in memory to my father's death in Arizona. When I arrived from Europe, I was too late to hold his ashes. I went into the dark and wrote. I followed the image and kept writing. Here is the poem "Cinquefoil" from the first chapter.

153

Cinquefoil

I hold in the palm of my hand a little yellow flower, a cinquefoil. The five petals form a mandala around the inner circle of seeds. My gaze is drawn to the center then out again to each petal. The flower weighs nothing, as light as air.

My father's ashes were as light as air, scattered in the courtyard before my arrival. I could not hold them in my hand. I entered the church and wept. My father in each tear. His melanoma surrounded by moist earth.

The petals curl and shrivel. My father always said, "Go do it." But now the doing is toppling me over. The flower needs to rest its head. My father's ashes are light, light as my flower. But his seeds are planted deep. (Circling to the Center, 7)

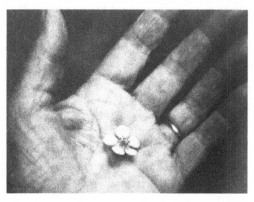

Cinquefoil

I wrote chapter after chapter of dark episodes in my life. By the time I arrived at the fifth chapter, the fifth petal, my little cinquefoil had turned into the golden flower. Here now is the poem "Golden Flower" from the fifth chapter.

Golden Flower

I sit at my desk and look at the photo of the golden flower. Innumerable cup-shaped petals cluster around the center. They open ever so slightly. Deep yellow spills over my desk, over my journal. For but an instant I hold gold in my hands.

When I was child, I looked for magic butter-cups in the fields. I would pick the most perfect one and place it close to my skin. If the deep yellow tinted my skin gold, it was a magic one. I'd hurry home, carrying my flower like a chalice.

The flower above my desk is a double butter-cup. I found it in the darkness deep within my heart. The fallow ground needed to be broken. The roots needed water, the leaves needed light. But there it flourished, a flower on God's altar. (idem, 93)

Double Buttercup

The transformation of the flower. Alchemy teaches us that when we give our attention to the darkness, it gives us in return new understanding. It reveals its hidden light. I followed my cinquefoil into the dark, into the alchemical furnace. I washed it and brought it out into the light. And lo, the small cinquefoil became the golden flower.

As writers, we look at alchemy as a way to deepen our creativity. Instead of lumps of earth and quicksilver, we use our lives and imagination. Our stories are the gold. First, we find the experience that calls out to be shared. We reimagine the experience and follow it into the unknown. We enter *nigredo*, the darkening. We go into darkness. Whether it be C.G. Jung, Atwood or Brodsky, we are all alchemists.

Let it become a practice. Remember Philemon's response to Jung that magic is reborn with each one of us. As writers, we turn inward. And, Atwood reminds us, the well of inspiration is a hole that leads downward. We dip into the well always more deeply, washing away the impurities. We hope with Brodsky that time will come when our passage through life will be flooded with light.

A writing suggestion:

Remember the experience of going into the dark that you wrote about. Was there a ray of light? Write about it. If not, imagine one and write a few lines. Be an alchemist.

In conclusion, I turn back to Jung's commentary to *The Secret of the Golden Flower.* Jung's purpose in writing the commentary was to build a bridge of psychological understanding between East and West, to emphasize the agreement between the symbolisms of East and West. "*It is a striving common to all civilized peoples. It is the tremendous experiment of becoming conscious, which nature has laid* upon mankind, and which unites the most diverse cultures in a common task. (The Secret of the Golden Flower, 136) The alchemists have shared their secrets. They have given us the steps to finding the Philosopher's Stone within. Nature calls us to respond.

Chapter Seven

Learning Zen: Clear Seeing, Clear Writing

"Zen frees us, enabling us to wake up and
become aware of our true nature."
D.T. Suzuki

"Jung drew parallels between what he saw as the Western
and Eastern approaches to achieving wholeness of personality
as exemplified by Zen Buddhism."
Sonu Shamdasani, *C.G. Jung's Library*

When Jung read *The Secret of the Golden Flower*, not only was he motivated to further his study of alchemy as described in Chapter Six, but also to deepen his study of Eastern philosophy and religion. Here was a culture that goes back thousands of years and that grew out of primitive instincts and that teaches detachment. The Western culture, on the other hand, was younger, especially the European and American, and more directed toward conquest. Two different worlds. Jung turned to the Orient to learn from the treasures of Eastern spirituality, namely Zen Buddhism.

Before looking at the parallels that Jung discovered between the practice of Zen and his own psychoanalytical practice, we will look at the history of Zen, including Jung's encounter with Izdubar in *The Red Book*. Then we will study two components of Zen, clear seeing and clear writing, with excerpts from Jung, from past and present Zen masters, including both D.T. Suzuki and S. Suzuki, also Tich Nhat Hanh, Natalie Goldberg, and Dinty W. Moore. We will practice clear seeing and clear writing.

1. Introduction and History of Zen

The word Zen is derived from the Japanese *zazen*, meaning to sit and meditate, and from the Chinese *ch'an* which is derived from the Sanskrit *dhyana*, meaning also to meditate. Its practice therefore goes from Japan back to China and from China back to India. To start in the beginning, we go to the origins of Buddhism in the sixth century B.C.E. with Siddhartha Gautama in northeastern India. The word comes from *budhi*, to awaken. Siddhartha became enlightened at the age of 35, overcame suffering, and spent the rest of his life teaching the way to true happiness. Over the centuries Buddhism developed into a religion and arrived in China in the first century C.E. where it encountered two powerful traditions: Confucianism and Taoism.

Confucianism may be described as an ethical philo- sophy developed from the teachings of the sage Confucius, 551-479 B.C.E. Confucius's hero was the duke of Zhou, 12th century B.C.E., who refined the feudal ritual system. The spiritual focus of Confucianism is on this world, the society, and the family, not on gods and afterlife. The teachings strive toward the cultivation of virtue.

Taoism is a religious philosophy based on the writings of Lao Tzu, the sixth century B.C.E. legendary philosopher and writer, reputed author of the *Tao Te Ching*. It strives toward living in harmony with the *Tao*, the way, the real, the indefinable. Its historical spokesman was Chuang Tzu, fourth century Taoist thinker and writer.

The Chinese mentality responded positively to the impact of Indian Buddhism and developed a special kind of spiritual discipline called Ch'an, broadly meaning meditation. It was not defined until the sixth century C.E. when the famed

Bodhidharma went to China and put forth the four truths to describe Chan Buddhism.

A special transmission outside the scriptures
Not founded upon words and letters,
Pointing directly to the human mind,
Seeing into one's nature and attaining
Buddhahood.

These four truths are still recognized today as the pillars of Zen Buddhism. (1) There are no scriptures. (2) The teaching is passed down from master to disciple. (3) Zen points directly at the mind, sometimes translated as the heart. (4) And is a way to Buddhahood, to the experience of *satori*, meaning sudden enlightenment.

From China, *Ch'an* traveled to Japan and was adopted by the Japanese in the 12ᵗʰ century under the name of Zen.

Master and Disciple

There are two Japanese Zen schools of thought. The Rinzai school emphasizes the importance of *satori* and teaches by *koans*, meaning riddles, mind teasers. The Soto school, on the other hand, emphasizes *zazen,* the practice of sitting still. Many of the Zen centers today practice both and try to avoid categorizing.

It was D.T. Suzuki, 1869-1966, who brought Zen to the West. He first traveled to America in 1908. Then returned in 1949 to teach for eight years at Columbia University. He was followed by another important Zen master, Shunryu Suzuki, 1905-1971, who went to the States in 1958 and founded the San Francisco Zen Center, where he continued to teach until his death.

Today, there are millions of Zen followers around the world. To many, it has become a way of living. Jung, in his Foreword to D.T. Suzuki's book *Introduction to Zen Buddhism,* wrote that Zen is the most important fruit that has sprung from the tree of Buddhism, whose root is the Flower Sermon of Buddha. This sermon was silent. It was the disciple Mahakasyapa's smile when Siddhartha Gautama held up a white flower in his silent sermon that signified the direct transmission of wisdom without words.

D.T. Suzuki writes, "Zen in its essence is the art of seeing into the nature of one's own being and points the way from bondage to freedom." (*Zen Buddhism, Selected Writings of D.T. Suzuki, 3*). Zen opens the way to enlightenment. It enables us to wake up and become aware.

> *When a certain moment is reached a hitherto closed screen is lifted, an entirely new vista opens up, and the tone of one's whole life thereafter changes. This mental opening is called satori by Zen masters. (idem, 91)*

How does *satori* happen? How does the closed screen in our mind suddenly lift? Suzuki relates dozens of examples from the different Zen masters throughout the centuries. He writes that these are matters of everyday occurrence. Here is one example from the ninth century. Tokusan, the great scholar of the Diamond Sutra, in learning that there was such a thing as Zen which ignores all the written sutras, comes for instruction from the Zen Master Ryutan. One day when Tokusan is sitting outside, trying to see into the mystery of Zen, Master Rhutan asks, "Why don't you come in?" Tokusan replies, "It is pitch dark." A candle is lit and handed over to him. Just as he is ready to take it, Master Ryutan blows out the light, at which point the mind of Tokusan opens.

We rest perplexed in reading this. What new way of viewing is this? How can blowing out a candle lead to the experience of *satori?* Then a screen in our mind lifts. The scales over our eyes fall away. And we smile.

Jung's Encounter with Izdubar in *The Red Book*

To enter into the mystery of Zen, we must let go of our points of reference. We must accept to enter into darkness. To blow out the candle. Only then will we be able to lift the lid of our conscious minds. This is indeed what Jung did in letting himself drop into the dark in 1913, into his confrontation with the unconscious. Unknowingly, he was following a similar path as that of the Eastern sages, which he would discover years later in reading the Taoist text *The Secret of the Golden Flower*.

During this confrontation, as we have seen, Jung realized he had lost his soul. He reached out for her hand, asking her to guide him. He called up fantasies, different figures some real others invented, and questioned them, writing long commentaries as he sought to understand the meaning of each experience. In the First Book, he encounters Elijah, the prophet of the Old Testament, and Salome, the dancer who asked for John the Baptist's head. He encounters also the serpent who will follow along on the journey. In the Second Book, he encounters among others, the Red Knight, Ammonius the Anchorite, the Librarian, and then Izdubar.

His encounter with Izdubar is a striking prefiguration of his actual turning to the study of Eastern philosophy. In his vision, Jung is going Eastward to look for the light he is lacking. At the top of a mountain pass, he meets the giant Izdubar (now known as Gilgamesh, semi-mythic King of Uruk in Sumeria.) While Jung is going Eastward, Izdubar is going Westward to find the birthplace of the sun. Jung relates the frightful encounter:

> *As I reach the pass, I see an enormous man approach from the other side. Two bull horns rise from his great head, a rattling suit of armor covers his chest. The giant is carrying a sparkling double axe.... I call out to him.*
> *I: "Oh Izdubar, most powerful, spare my life"*
> *Iz: "I do not want your life. Where do you come from?"....*
> *I: "I come from a Western land whose coast washes against the great Western sea."*
> *Iz: "Does the sun sink in that sea? Or does it touch the solid land in its decline?"*
> *I: "The sun sinks far beyond the sea."*
> *Iz: "Beyond the sea? What lies there?"*
> *I: "There is nothing but empty space. As you know, the earth is round and turns around the sun.*
> *Iz: "So there is no immortal land where the sun goes down to be reborn. Are you speaking the truth?" His eyes flicker with fury and fear.*

*I: "I'm really speaking the truth.... In so far as
you are mortal, you can never reach the sun."
Iz: "I shall never reach the sun, and never
reach immortality?" He smashes his axe. "Be
gone, miserable weapon...." He collapses and
sobs like a child.... "Have you no Gods
anymore?"
I: "No, words are all we have."
Iz: "We do not have Gods either and yet we
believe that they exist. We recognize their
workings in natural events."
I: "Science has taken from us the capacity of
belief.... For that reason, I've set out to the
East, to the land of the rising sun, to seek the
light that we lack." (The Red Book, 278)*

Jung is speaking here for the Western mind, where science rules the day. Izdubar is speaking for the Eastern mind, where the Gods rule the day. Jung acknowledges that the West has lost its Gods. It has only words. When Izdubar realizes that he will never reach the sun, never reach immortality, he smashes his ax and falls to the ground as if paralyzed. The story continues but we stop here.

In summoning imaginary figures and entering into dialogue with them, Jung was letting go of his intellect. He was developing the technique that he later called active imagination that would lead him along the path of *wu wei*—action by nonaction—followed by the Eastern sages in *The Secret of the Golden Flower*.

We can now appreciate the magnitude of his realization that the content of this Chinese text was a living parallel to what he was witnessing in his own psychic development and in that of his patients. The analogy between various myth-motifs and symbols showed a common substratum of the psyche that transcends all differences in culture and consciousness. Jung defines his stubstratum as the collective unconscious in his Commentary to *The Secret of the Golden Flower.*

> *I have called this substratum the collective unconscious. This unconscious psyche, common to all mankind, does not consist merely of contents capable of becoming conscious, but of latent dispositions towards certain identical reactions.... Thus the various lines of psychic development start from one common stock, whose roots reach back into all the strata of the past. (Commentary, The Secret of the Golden Flower, 87)*

In our Taoist text, the creation of the higher consciousness, of the superior personality, is what is meant by the golden flower. As Master Lü-tsu teaches, the light rotates on its own if one accepts what comes to one. "It is a question of yea-saying to oneself, of taking one's self as the most serious of tasks, of being conscious of everything one does." (idem, 95) In the years ahead, Jung will immerse himself in Indian and Chinese texts as he draws parallels between Eastern and Western approaches to achieving wholeness, to what the Eastern sages call the experience of *satori,* or enlightenment.

In 1935, Jung wrote a psychological commentary to *The Tibetan Book of the Dead,* in which he expresses his high esteem for the work. Jung saw in the book an initiation process to restore to the soul the divinity that it lost at birth, a process not unlike the work of individuation, the striving toward wholeness. For years, the *Bardo Thödol* had been his constant companion. He owed to it not only many stimulating ideas and discoveries but also many fundamental insights.

Later, in 1949, he wrote the foreword to *The I Ching, The Book of Changes,* in which he tested the correspondence between the Taoist thinking about interrelatedness and his own thinking about synchronicity, the acausal principle behind meaningful circumstances. If we put ourselves in the Tao, if we enter our true being, life has its own answer. "Like a part of nature, it [*The I Ching*] waits until it is discovered. It offers neither facts nor power, but for lovers of self-knowledge, of wisdom—if there be such—it seems to be the right book." (*Foreword,* xxxix)

It is in letting things happen in the psyche that Jung was able to discover these parallels between the Eastern mind and the Western mind. Before looking at length at clear seeing and clear writing, let's pause and ask ourselves what Zen means to us.

A writing suggestion:
Imagine yourself with a Zen master and ask him what is Zen. Maybe write this in the form of a dialogue. Blow out the candle. Let yourself be surprised.

2. Clear Seeing

Both clear seeing and clear writing demonstrate the purpose of Zen to let go and get back to the direct experience of life. In order to directly experience life, Zen focuses on what is in front of us. A Zen mind is like a mirror. When a mirror reflects a tree, there is only the tree in the reflection. There aren't other trees in the reflection, or bushes, or people. When a Zen mind sees a tree, there is only the tree. When a

Zen mind sees a white flower, there is only the white flower. D.T. Suzuki wrote "Zen in its essence is the art of seeing."

John C.H. Wu

Let's look at two different 20th-century thinkers and authors, then again at C.G. Jung, to appreciate how the three saw Zen as the experience of clear seeing. First John C.H. Wu (1899-1986) a Chinese scholar and lawyer, a Taoist who converted to Catholicism, fled from Communist rule, taught at Seton Hall College in New Jersey, retired as a Senator in Taiwan. John Wu brought to the world a lived experience and understanding of Taoism, Confucianism, Zen, and Christianity. He translated the *Tao Te Ching* into English and the New Testament into Chinese, rendering the prologue to the Gospel of John, "In the beginning was the Tao." He never gave up his early Chinese roots, which led him to write *The Golden Age of Zen* in 1967, in an effort to introduce the great Zen masters of the seventh to 10th centuries to the Western world.

John C.H. Wu saw *satori* (enlightenment) with both Eastern eyes and Western eyes. It is the same enlightenment, be it experienced by a Zen master or a Christian mystic. He wrote that with practice, Zen opened the way to higher consciousness and to deeper goodness. With practice, we are freed from our controlling ego and our persistence to conceptualize the truth.

> *Zen emphasizes the intuitive perception of truth as the way to enlightenment and also the un-expected experience of spontaneous goodness. Such goodness liberates you from the shell of your little ego and from the stuffy realm of concepts to the beyond. (Golden Age of Zen, 205)*

I was fortunate to experience this spontaneous goodness in 1957, when Wu was teaching at Seton Hall. I had an
assignment to interview him for Pax Romana about his
recently translated book *Beyond East and West.* I was to drive
to his home, with my French fiancé, for an appointment in
midafternoon. On the way, there was a freak snowstorm that
stalled traffic for hours and made it impossible to move on
the turnpike. I dared to knock on his door hours past the time.
He welcomed us with warm eagerness and led us to the dining
room where his wife and 13 children were sitting around the
large round table. They all stood to greet us and add two more
places. We would join them and do the interview after the
meal. "There will be time this way to clear the roads," he
assured us. Zen.

As we learn to let go, we learn to truly see. Wu relates
many stories of clear seeing. I have chosen one of them.

> *One master came to his enlightenment on seeing
> the peach blossoms. "Ever since I saw the peach
> blossoms, I had no more doubts." Of course he
> had seen peach blossoms previously but it was
> only on that occasion that he really saw them,
> saw them not as isolated objects but as lively
> spurts from the source of the whole universe.
> (idem, 212)*

To see the peach blossoms. To see them as spouts from
the source of the universe. Here today, gone tomorrow. When
we really see the peach blossoms, the distance between the
blossoms and ourselves disappears. We experience an at-
oneness with nature.

Here where I live, when I see—when I really see—the
ginkgo tree down the road, its blossoming branches against
the blue sky, the distance between the yellow laden branches

Blossoming Ginkgo Tree

and myself disappears. I feel the same oneness. I am one with the tree and its flowering branches.

When I walk by the ginkgo tree, laden with blossoms, this perception of the oneness of the creation takes me back to the evening with John Wu and lets me live anew the spontaneous goodness of humankind.

Thomas Merton

During his years in America, John Wu received a request from a Trappist monk who wanted Wu's guidance in translating poems of Chuang Tzu, Taoist poet of the sixth century B.C.E. The monk was Thomas Merton, whom I wrote about in Chapters One and Five. Wu responded to Merton, writing that he had been waiting for Merton to take the initiative, believing that their friendship was fated. So began a friendship that lasted for seven years until Merton's tragic death in 1968. Wu guides Merton into writing *The Way of Chuang Tzu,* and Merton writes an introduction to Wu's *The Golden Age of Zen.* Wu was delighted to discover a monk who grasped the spirit of Zen "as well as an ancient master," a monk who built "a living bridge between East and West."

In his Introduction, Merton writes that Zen is a way of being. We step out of our narrow-mindedness and enter a universal space.

> *Zen is consciousness unstructured by a parti-*
> *cular form, a trans-cultural, trans-religious,*
> *trans-formed consciousness. It wants to get back*
> *to the direct experience of life without logical*
> *verbalizing.... We quickly forget how to simply*
> *see things and substitute our words and our*
> *formulas for the things themselves so that we see*
> *only what conveniently fits our prejudices.*
> *(Merton, Introduction, The Golden Age of Zen,*
> *4, 49)*

Merton, once he received the authorization to move into his hermitage in the middle of the woods at Gethsemani Monastery, was able to fully practice clear seeing. He spent long days sitting on his porch, watching the redbuds blossom, walking in the woods, seeing a mother deer protect her young ones, feasting his eyes on everything around him. And he wrote about it in his journal.

> *November 4, In the afternoon, there were lots of*
> *pretty little myrtle warblers, playing and diving*
> *for insects in the low pine branches over my*
> *head.... I was awed at their loveliness, their*
> *quick flight, their lookings and chirpings. A*
> *sense of total kinship with them as if they and I*

were all of the same nature and as if that nature
were nothing but love. (A Vow of Conversation,
95)

In clear seeing, Merton was living the oneness of creation. In another of his innumerable books, titled *Zen and the Birds of Appetite*, he specifically encourages us to experience this oneness. We only have to start looking.

If one reaches the point where understanding
fails, this is not a tragedy; it is simply a
reminder to stop thinking and start looking.
Perhaps there is nothing to figure out after all;
perhaps we only need to wake up." (Zen and the
Birds of Appetite, 53)

On his one trip to Asia, he experienced his final waking up. He was in Sri Lanka, at Polonnaruwa, alone, walking barefoot along the wooded paths to the temple of Buddha, where there are the four colossal rock relief statues of the Buddha.

December 4, 1968, Colombo
Looking at these figures I was suddenly, almost
forcibly, jerked clean out of the habitual, half-
tied vision of things, and an inner clearness,
clarity, as if exploding from the rocks themselves,
became evident and obvious.... The rock, all
matter, all life, is charged with dharmakaya [the
essence of all things].
I have now seen and have pierced through the
surface and have got beyond the shadow and the
disguise. This is Asia in its purity...complete. It
says everything; it needs nothing.

The whole thing is very much a Zen garden, a
span of bareness and openness and evidence and
the great figures, motionless, yet with the lines
in full movement, waves of vesture and bodily
form, a beautiful and holy vision." (The Asian
Journal, 233-34)

Six days later, Merton died, electrocuted by faulty
wiring of a fan. He had just given a lecture on Marxism and
monasticism to an international assembly of monks in
Bangkok, underlining the monk's unique pursuit, "the monk
is seeking to change man's consciousness." His pursuit had
been answered, I believe, at Polonnaruwa. Merton's legacy
continues to shine.

C.G. Jung

It is through clear seeing that John C.H. Wu and
Thomas Merton experienced this inner awakening that Zen
Buddhists call *satori*. It was likewise for Jung. Among the
many moments of clear seeing and inner awakenings that
Jung experienced, I single out a few.

First, we remember his experience as a young child of
seeing the waves on Lake Constance, washed up to the shore,
glistening in the sunlight. He could not be dragged away from
the water, from the shore of the lake. He was still a very young
child, but he remembers feeling an inconceivable pleasure.
Seeing an incomparable splendor. An early inner awakening.

We saw also in Chapter Five, how the sea continued to
be a source of emerging awareness throughout Jung's life, as
witnessed in his letter to his wife, Emma, while traveling to
the States in 1909. "The sea is like music; it has all the dreams
of the soul within itself." Here is another letter to Emma,
written later during his first travels to North Africa.

Sousse, Monday, March 15, 1920
Unfortunately I cannot write coherently to you,
for it is all too much. Only sidelights. After cold,
heavy weather at sea, a sparkling morning in
Algiers. Bright houses and streets, dark green
clumps of trees, tall palms rising among them....
You no longer think of yourself; you are
dissolved in this potpourri which cannot be
evaluated, still less described...
Imagine a tremendous sun, air clear as in the
highest mountains, a sea bluer than any you
have ever seen, all colors of incredible power.
(MDR, 403)

Jung can only stammer. He can no longer think of himself. He writes that he does not know what Africa is really saying to him, but it speaks. It speaks because Jung is practicing clear seeing. The sea is bluer than Emma has ever seen.

Later, in 1925, there is the inner awakening that Jung experienced in seeing the sunrise in Kenya, when everything in the dark valley turned to flaming crystal. Jung found himself like inside a temple. There were more travels, more letters, more moments of clear seeing.

Then, after his wife's death, when he retreated to the Tower at Bollingen, on the shore of the Zurich Sea, he often felt not sudden moments of awakening, but rather a longer, fully appreciated time of deep awareness. It was here where he felt he was living his true life, where he was most deeply himself. Where from the inner courtyard, he could look out on the water.

At Bollingen, silence surrounds me almost
audibly, and I live "in modest harmony with

Doorway to the Sea, The Tower

nature." [title of an old Chinese woodcut showing a little old man in a heroic landscape] Thoughts rise to the surface which reach back into the centuries, and accordingly anticipate a remote future. Here the torment of creation is lessened; creativity and play are close together. (idem, 253)

Jung has listened to Eastern wisdom. In his Foreword to Suzuki's *Introduction to Zen Buddhism,* Jung writes that Zen is an experience of transformation. "It is not that something different is seen, but that one sees differently." One sees differently because one is different. Clear seeing brings transformation.

175

A writing suggestion:
Stay with clear seeing for a moment. Imagine a white flower. Or imagine whatever flower comes to you. Look at it for a few minutes. Write about what you see.

3. Clear Writing

I turn now to clear writing. To show how clear writing comes with clear seeing. When we write from our authentic self, there is a vibration and clarity in our words. We address the reader directly. There is no one, no thing, in between. Let me give a few examples of clear writing from 20th-century practitioners of Zen, and again returning to Jung.

Shunryu Suzuki

I turn to the second Suzuki to bring Zen to the States, Shunryu Suzuki, whom I mentioned in my short overview of Zen Buddhism. S. Suzuki wrote that to practice Zen, we need beginner's mind. Shunryu Suzuki was a direct spiritual descendent from the 13th-century Zen master Dogen. He drew his teaching from this source, believing it could be as meaningful to the West as it has been to the East. His book *Zen Mind, Beginner's Mind* originated in a series of talks that he gave at his Zen Center in Los Altos, California. Let us listen.

> *The goal of practice is always to keep our beginner's mind.... Our 'original mind' includes everything within itself. This does not mean a closed mind, but actually an empty mind and a ready mind. If your mind is empty, it is always ready for anything; it is open to everything. In*

*the beginner's mind there are many possibilities;
in the expert's mind there are few. (Zen Mind,
Beginner's Mind, 21)*

Beginner's Mind is a kind of mind that sees things as they are. That finds words that are simple and straightforward. That focuses attention uniquely on what it wants to express. Shunryu Suzuki gives an example of beginner's mind in the following quote from his master, Dogen-zenai.

Dogen-zenai said, 'Even though it is midnight, dawn is here; even though dawn comes, it is night-time.' Nighttime and daytime are not different. The same thing is sometimes called nighttime, sometimes called daytime. They are one thing. (idem, p. 118)

The Zen saying is paradoxical yet in very few words, clearly written, it exposes the error of dualism and the correctness of oneness. Midnight and dawn, nighttime and daytime are one if we keep beginner's mind.

Shunryu Suzuki concludes his book with his own paradoxical words.

Before the rain stops we hear a bird. Even under the heavy snow we see snowdrops and some new growth. (idem, 138)

Everything is movement, everything is one. If we practice clear hearing, before the rain stops, the bird is already singing. And clear seeing, then before the snow melts, there is greenery.

Thich Nhat Hanh

Following in this path of clear seeing and clear writing, there is the Vietnamese Zen monk and peace activist Thich Nhat Hanh, who received the "lamp transmission" to be a Zen master in 1966. He studied at Princeton, taught Buddhism at Columbia in the early 1960s. He met with both Martin Luther King and Thomas Merton who penned the essay "Nhat Hanh Is My Brother." Since 1982, he has lived in Plum Village, a Zen center in Dordogne, in southern France. He has authored innumerable books, including *Cultivating the Mind of Love*, subtitled *The Practice of Looking Deeply in the Mahayana Buddhist Tradition.*

Nhat Hanh writes with a clear mind and masterful simplicity. He teaches the concept of mindfulness, to let go of our thoughts and concerns, so as to be mindful only of the present moment. In *Cultivating the Mind of Love,* he interweaves moments of his own formation with Buddhist texts to show us ways to cultivate our own mind of love. His sincere, natural way of presenting Buddhist concepts opens the door for the reader to enter the realm of Zen. Here is an example:

> *In the Snake Sutra, the Buddha tells us that the Dharma [teaching] is a raft we can use to cross the river and get to the other shore. But after we have crossed the river, if we continue to carry the raft on our shoulders, that would be foolish. (Cultivating the Mind of Love, 28)*

Nhat Hanh continues, it would best to leave the raft on the water's edge for someone else to use in the same way. We listen easily. And we remember easily.

Nhat Hanh concludes *Cultivating the Mind of Love* with a lesson in seeing. One autumn day as he was practicing walking meditation, the leaves were falling like the rain. He stepped on a leaf, picked it up, looked at it and smiled. He realized that the leaf has always been there. It falls in autumn and remanifests itself in the spring.

> *When I looked deeply into the leaf, I saw it was not just one leaf, just as the Buddha is not just one person. The Buddha is, at the same time, everywhere. The leaf, too, was everywhere. Because the leaf was free from notions of birth and death, it was able to do so. (idem, 115-116)*

When we look at the flowers, trees, and children with the eyes of compassion, we transform all life. Nhat Hanh teaches that compassion is born of understanding, and understanding is born of looking deeply. When we look deeply, we write deeply. So it is when Nhat Hanh turns to poetry. Here is the opening stanza from his poem "Walking Joyfully in the Ultimate Dimension."

> Walking joyfully in the ultimate dimension
> walk with your feet, not with your head.
> If you walk with your head, you'll get lost. (idem,120)

The ultimate dimension is complete freedom, peace, and joy. Nhat Han refers to this dimension as the ground of being. For many of us, we hear an echo of Meister Eckhart's teaching about the same ground, *der Seele Grund,* the ground of the soul, the source of all being. Whether we be Eastern sages or Western mystics, whether we be Nhat Hanh or Thomas Merton, the ultimate dimension is one.

Natalie Goldberg

One of Nhat Hanh's pupils is Natalie Goldberg, the esteemed Zen Buddhist author and speaker, best-known for her series of books on the craft of writing. She wrote the Foreword to *Cultivating the Mind of Love,* after having spent a long retreat at Plum Village, where she listened to Nhat Hanh give the Dharma talks that comprise the book.

> *I am continually amazed at how Thich Nhat Hanh is able to translate the Buddhist tradition into everyday life and make it relevant and helpful for so many people. (Cultivating the Mind of Love, vii)*

It was during this retreat that she started to see the parallels between the work of a Zen master and the work of a writer. Clarity was the key.

> *I realized then that the work of a Zen master is also the work of a writer—to take nothing for granted but to live deeply and feel the life we have been given. It is also the work of everyone if we are to bring peace to this world. It is our chance to glimpse the interconnected nature of all things. (idem, ix)*

Following her best-selling book, *Writing Down the Bones*, *Freeing the Writer Within,* she continued teaching writing, opening the minds of her students and audiences to our inner source of creativity. After 15 years, she wanted to hand on what she had learned from her practice of Zen meditation. She wrote *Wild Mind, Living the Writer's Life.*

> *What writing practice, like Zen practice, does is*
> *bring you back to the natural state of mind, the*
> *wilderness of your mind where there are no*
> *refined rows of gladiolas. The mind is raw, full*
> *of energy, alive and hungry. It does not think in*
> *the way we were brought up to think—well-*
> *mannered, congenial." (Wild Mind, xiii)*

We need to awaken our wild minds. Being a writer is a whole way of life, a way of seeing, a way of being. Like Zen masters, writers hand on what they know.

Dinty W. Moore

Another example of clear writing comes from Dinty W. Moore, author of several books of fiction and nonfiction, professor of creative writing at Ohio University. In his lifelong pursuit of writing and creativity, Moore opened to the path of Buddhism and grew aware of the simple wisdom of mindfulness. In one of his recent books, *The Mindful Writer,* to show how writing and mindfulness intersect, Moore offers a series of quotations from a wide selection of writers and artists followed by brief responses to illustrate their convergence.

Here is how Moore responds to the quote from George Saunders, "Stay open, forever, so open it hurts, and then open up some more."

> *Look at a child, maybe two years old, wide-eyes,*
> *full of wonder, amazed by the smallest thing—a*
> *yellow butterfly, a smooth rock, a stranger's*
> *smile—or, in an instant, ready to bawl at the*
> *world's pain and injustice.*

> *Look at the average adult: jaded, seen-it-all,*
> *skeptical, ready to dismiss his own feelings as*
> *false because his intellect is trying to damp down*
> *the emotions....*
> *When I am writing well, I'm closer to that*
> *first person, the child fresh in the moment,*
> *surprised by everything because I am seeing*
> *anew. (The Mindful Writer, 130-131)*

Moore asks us to see the rock, the butterfly, the smile, as if we are seeing it for the first time. And are we willing to bawl at the world's injustice? Mindfulness means simply being open to what is directly before us.

C.G. Jung

Clear seeing and clear writing. So it was for Jung when he wrote *Memories, Dreams, Reflections*. It was late in his life. He was dictating the book to his colleague Aniela Jaffé. Then taken up into the mystique of writing, he continued on his own. The writing itself is beautiful. We pause for a moment to remember that we are reading an English translation and to recognize the important and precious work of translators.

If we go back and look at the examples of clear seeing given earlier in this chapter, we cannot help but appreciate the clear writing. Let us consider another excerpt, this time from his voyage in India in 1938. Jung is describing here his visit to the stupas of Sanchi, there where Buddha delivered his fire sermon.

> *I was overcome by a strong emotion of the kind*
> *that frequently develops in me when I encounter*
> *a thing, person, or idea of whose significance I*
> *am still unconscious. The stupas are situated on*

> *a rocky hill whose peak can be reached by a*
> *pleasant path of great stone slabs laid down*
> *through a green meadow. (MDR, 308)*

Jung describes how he walked through one of four elaborate gates. The path then turned left and led into a circumambulation around the stupa. When he finished one circumambulation, he entered a second one. At this moment, he was overcome with emotion.

> *The distant prospect over the plain, the stupas*
> *themselves, the temple ruins, and the solitary*
> *stillness of this holy site held me in a spell. I took*
> *leave of my companion and submerged myself in*
> *the overpowering mood of the place. (ibid.)*

It was in this state of reverie that he heard rhythmic gong tones approaching. A group of Japanese pilgrims came marching up one behind the other, each striking a small gong, beating out the rhythm of the age-old prayer *Om mani padme hum.*

> *Outside the stupas they bowed low, then passed*
> *through the gate. There they bowed again before*
> *the statue of the Buddha, intoning a chorale-like*
> *song. (ibid.)*

They completed the double circumambulation, singing a hymn before each statue of Buddha.

> *As I watched them, my mind and spirit were with*
> *them, and something within me silently thanked*
> *them for having so wonderfully come to the aid*
> *of my inarticulate feelings....*

> *A new side of Buddhism was revealed to me there. I grasped the life of the Buddha as the reality of the self which had broken through and laid claim to a personal life. (idem, 309)*

From this experience of seeing, this inner awakening, so clearly transcribed, Jung understood that for Buddha, the self stands above all gods and represents the essence of human existence and of the world as a whole.

Before concluding this chapter on Zen, I turn to the Introduction of my book *One Year to a Writing Life* where I write about the source of our writing. The source lies within us and is the same creative source, the same one deep well, in all spiritual traditions. When we tap into it, we find our words. But we must do so in a Zen fashion, remembering the importance of full attention. Not letting our minds interfere.

> *If the well is blocked, the water does not rise. But if we clear away the clutter, our creativity over-flows and touches those around us. Inspiration is breathing. We breathe in, we dip into the well for water. We breathe out, we carry the water with us. We do this with words, finding our stories in the dark and sharing them in the light. (One Year to a Writing Life, xix)*

We find our words within us. But first we need to clear away the clutter, all the buzz, the noise, the television, the computer, the iPhone. We have to practice zen. Clear seeing. Then clear writing as we carry our words with us, out to the world around us.

A writing suggestion:

Write with beginner's mind a journal entry or maybe a poem about seeing a white flower, a ginkgo tree, or another image. Close your eyes, see the flower or the tree, then put a few words on paper. No thinking, no judging. Dip into the well and be surprised.

In conclusion, let us look at a koan that sums up seamlessly this lesson in Zen. But as Meister Eckhart taught us, we have to break the shell to get the kernel.

> *A Zen Master said to his disciple: "Go get my rhinoceros horn fan."*
> *Disciple: "Sorry, Master, it is broken."*
> *Master: "Okay, then get me the rhinoceros."*
> *(Thomas Merton, Zen and the Birds of Appetite, 14)*

Learning Zen is entering into the unknowing. It's fetching the rhinoceros. It's reaching down into the well within us. Confronting the unconscious. Seeing the peach blossom. Discovering a kinship with all that surrounds us. Living the oneness of creation. It's clear seeing, clear writing.

Chapter Eight

Writing Toward Wholeness: Cultivating the Self

"The attainment of wholeness requires one to stake
one's whole being. Nothing less will do."
C.G. Jung

"There is something in the depths of our being
that hungers for wholeness."
Thomas Merton

Wholeness had been the goal of spiritual seekers from earliest times. How has the concept of wholeness been perceived throughout the centuries? We will learn from Hestia, the Goddess of the Hearth, then from Lao Tzu, and Plato, moving forward in time to Julian of Norwich. What did these seekers mean by "wholeness"? We will then turn to Jung, whose entire life was a journey toward wholeness, reading again from *The Red Book* and seeing how the different stages of his life gave physical shape to the Tower at Bollingen. He called the journey individuation, whereby the unconscious is brought into consciousness, to be assimilated into the whole personality, the self.

We will next turn to Thomas Merton, whose search for an underlying wholeness paralleled Jung's search. Then to help us answer this same longing in ourselves, we will read excerpts from contemporary authors Clarissa Pinkola Estés, Annie Dillard and Orhan Pamuk, all of whom write toward wholeness. We will see how to bring together the different parts of ourselves into the unique being that is our destiny. We will write toward wholeness.

1. What Is Wholeness?

Wholeness is the revelation of the oneness of everything. The oneness of humankind, the oneness of nature, the oneness of all creation. Such insight into the unity of all things is a state of grace found in all religions: Hinduism, Buddhism, Taoism, Zen, Christian mysticism, Jewish mysticism, Sufism. It is the seed that grows into something still larger than the mustard tree, the seed that grows into one global community living in peace on our planet.

This oneness is best seen in the unity of opposites, one of the oldest secrets of human existence. Consider the rainbow, an admixture of rain in sunshine. Opposites. How beautifully they come together. Think of music; it is the alteration of sound and silence. We need both, otherwise there is no music. And a great emotion. We experience an emotion of joy often with tears. Opposites.

Thomas Merton, the Trappist monk, in his essay "Herakleitos the Obscure," wrote, "True peace is the hidden attunement of opposite tensions—a paradox and a mystery transcending both sense and will, like the ecstasy of the mystic." (Pramuk, *Sophia,* 139) The attunement of opposites. Rain and sunshine, sound and silence, joy and tears, night and day. Without night, there is no day. Without one, there is no other.

As we look through history at figures who represent and spoke for wholeness, we could start with Hestia, the first born of Rhea and Cronos, and yet the least known of the major Greek gods and goddesses. Hestia guarded the hearth on Mount Olympus. The other gods and goddesses would leave Mount Olympus, would seek adventure and then return. Hestia would be waiting. The hearth of Hestia was kept burning in all the homes. Here is the Homeric prayer that was recited every morning,

> *Hestia, you who tend the holy house of the Lord Apollo…with soft oil dripping ever from your locks, come now into this house, come, having one mind with Zeus the all wise, draw near and withal bestow grace upon my song.*

Her round hearth is a mandala symbol, or sacred circle, depicting a state of harmony, of wholeness. At its center was a sacred fire, to which everything is related and which is in itself a source of energy. Hestia's hearth is a symbol of wholeness, the archetype of oneness that connects us to the essence of creation.

On the other side of the world, there was Lao Tzu (604-531 B.C.E.) and the *Tao Te Ching*. Tradition tells us that Lao Tzu was the learned keeper of the imperial archives at the ancient capital of Loyang. Seeing the decay of the society, he rode away to live alone in the desert. But at the Hanku Pass, he was stopped by a gatekeeper who begged him to set down in writing the core of his teaching. Let us appreciate his words in Chapter 28 in the *Tao Te Ching*:

> *Know the strength of man,*
> *But keep a woman's care!*

The *Tao Te Ching* speaks of an inner wholeness, the yin and yang. When together, they are the Tao. Lao Tzu invites us to bring these forces together in ourselves, masculine and feminine, light and darkness.

Two centuries later, back in Greece, we return to Plato's Symposium (380-375), this time to Aristophanes' speech about the human longing for wholeness. Several disciples of Socrates are discussing the nature of love. Aristophanes defines love as the longing for the other. He recounts this myth of the origins of human beings.

> *The primeval man was round, his back and sides forming a circle, and he had four hands and the same number of feet, one head with two faces.... Terrible was their might and strength, great were the thoughts of their hearts, and they made an attack upon the gods.... Doubt reigned in the celestial councils. At last after a good deal of reflection, Zeus discovered a way.*
>
> *"Me thinks I have a plan which will enfeeble their strength and so extinguish their turbulence; men shall continue to exist, but I will cut them in two...." He spoke and cut men in two, like a sorb-apple which is halved for pickling....*
>
> *This becoming one instead of two was the very expression of man's ancient need. And the reason is that human nature was originally one and we were a whole, and the desire and pursuit of the whole is called love. (Dialogues of Plato, The Symposium, par. 180-190)*

For Aristophanes, the search for the other was the search for our original oneness. Separated from our other half, we long for wholeness. We will always be looking for our missing half, for wholeness. "The desire and pursuit of the whole is called love."

As we move forward through the centuries, let us consider Julian of Norwich, in the 14th century, mystic, writer, and living as an anchoress, a solitary enclosed in an anchorage or vicarage engaging in a life of prayer. Her spiritual classic, *Revelations of Divine Love*, relating her visions or "showings," is a gospel of love. Julian's theology is one of integration. She saw the wholeness of God—Father, Mother, and Spirit—reflected in the creation.

> *So when he made us God almighty was our kindly Father, and God all-wise our kindly Mother, and the Holy Spirit their love and goodness.... In our Father, God almighty, we have our being. In our merciful Mother we have reformation and renewal, and our separate parts are integrated into perfect man. (Revelations of Divine Love, Edition 1966, 165)*

We have our being in the Father, our renewal in the Mother, and our different parts are integrated into one being. Julian called this integration "one-ing'. The one-ing of the creation with the Creator. Julian sees God's presence in all creation. Even in a small hazelnut that is given to her. She holds the hazelnut in the palm of her hand and writes,

> *I looked at the hazel nut with the eye of my understanding and thought, what can this be? I was amazed that it could last for I thought that because of its littleness it would suddenly have fallen into nothing. And I was answered in my understanding. It lasts and always will, because God loves it, and thus everything has being through the love of God. (idem, 68)*

In the littleness of the hazelnut, God showed Julian that the meaning of all creation is love. In our oneness with God, all shall be well. And it always shall be.

All shall be well, and all shall be well, and all manner of thing shall be well. (idem, Edition 1998, 80)

Julian, the 14th century anchoress arrived at a feeling of wholeness which let her say, "All shall be well." Let's pause to ask ourselves how we think about wholeness. How do we see wholeness?

A writing suggestion:

What does wholeness mean to you? What image of wholeness comes to you? A rainbow? A hazelnut? An oak tree? A child's face? Describe it in in few lines.

2. Jung's Life Quest for Wholeness

Jung throughout his life was searching for wholeness. As he wrote in his Foreword to Suzuki's *Introduction to Zen Buddhism,* "The attainment of wholeness requires one to stake one's whole being." Jung did just that in consciously bringing together the contraries that he experienced during his long life. Even during his early school years, he realized he had two personalities: number one, a typical Swiss schoolboy; and number two, an authoritative dignified man from the past. Sometimes he was number one, sometimes number two. Then, in midlife after breaking with Freud, the spirit of the depths called to him, overriding the spirit of this time.

Listening to the spirit of the depths, Jung went in search of his soul, his anima. After days in the desert, he saw his soul as a wispy maiden. He reached out to hold her hand, to

192

follow her. He meets Elijah, the Old Testament prophet representing logos, and his blind daughter Salome from the New Testament, representing eros. Shocked by this vision, of seeing Elijah and Salome living together, Jung is stunned into disbelief. Fear seizes him. He is surrounded by the dark night. We could see here an early foreshadowing of the *coniunctio* of logos and eros. Jung continues on his path, encountering different figures of his imagination, each representing a different part of his nature. He writes it all down, with his commentaries, and transcribes it into *The Red Book*, all the while looking to bring together his two personalities, which he now identifies as the ego and the self. It would be a lifetime quest.

This was Jung's path, widened to include the study of alchemy and of Eastern religions as well as his ongoing scientific research and psychoanalytical work with patients. His life was a journey into wholeness. He called it individuation. The coming together of the conscious psyche and the unconscious. The encounter of opposites, the process of making a connection between the ego and the images in the unconscious, in the realization of the self. The unending *coniunctio*.

His journey into wholeness is prefigured in the drawing of his first mandala, *Systema munditotius* (The System of All Worlds). Jung wrote on the back of the painting, "This is the first mandala I constructed in the year 1916, wholly unconscious of what it meant." In studying the details of the drawing, we see hints of the gigantic task that Jung saw ahead of him. The bringing together of opposites into the center. The finding of wholeness.

The mandala was first anonymously published in 1955, when Jung was 80 years old. He wrote the following comments.

> *It portrays the antinomies of the microcosm*
> *within the macrocosmic world and its antino-*
> *mies. At the very top the figure of a young boy in*
> *the winged egg called Phanes [Greek primordial*
> *God of creation and life].... His dark antithesis*
> *in the depths is here designated as Abraxas. He*
> *represents the dominus mundi, the lord of the*
> *physical world.... A further division is hori-*
> *zontal, to the left...the serpent which winds itself*
> *around the phallus as the generative principle....*
> *To the right, the dove of the Holy Ghost takes*
> *wing and wisdom Sophia pours from a double*
> *beaker, to left and right. (The Red Book, 364)*

Within the sphere that has the zigzag lines, the macro-cosm is repeated, but with the upper and lower regions reversed. The spheres keep repeating, and reversing, "endless in number, growing ever smaller until the innermost core, the actual microcosm is reached." At the center is a star or sun, representing a divine spark, a fragment of the pleroma, the ultimate oneness.

To attain oneness with this spark, we must transcend the opposites through an unending series of *coniunctios* , inner and outer, masculine and feminine, day and night, logos and eros, earth and heaven. This first mandala is a symbolic representation of the reconciliation of opposites. It may there-fore be seen as an embryo of Jung's process of individuation, leading to wholeness, to a unity with the Self.

The mandala was imagined and drawn the same year that Jung wrote *The Seven Sermons to the Dead*, an inspired piece of writing composed in three nights after a dramatic, parapsychological experience, when spirits of the dead appeared at Jung's door crying out, "We have come back from Jerusalem where we found not what we sought." The response

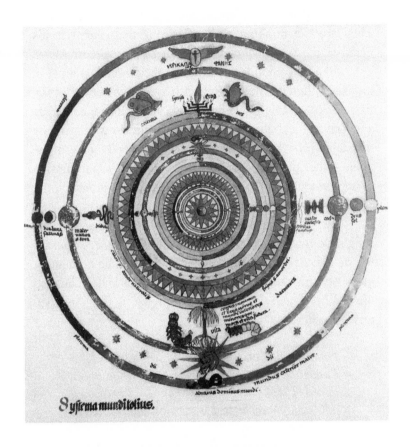

Systema munditotius, C.G. Jung, The Red Book

is given by Philemon, an imaginary Alexandrian Gnostic. This dialogue between Philemon and the dead is at the same time a dialogue between Jung and his unconscious. The sermons are included in the *Scrutinies*, third part of *The Red Book*. They are the thinking and reflections that elucidate his mandala, the *Systema munditotius*, Jung's psycho-cosmology.

I had the good fortune to hold the original painting in my hands, in the office of Robert Hinshaw, the editor of my first book, *Looking for Gold*. Aniela Jaffé, Jung's colleague and private secretary until his death, made a gift of the mandala to Hinshaw. As I held the painting and looked at the images, the spheres began to slowly spin and to turn upside down. I watched as they grew smaller and approached the center. May my words here express my gratefulness.

Let us now examine two of the dialogues that illustrate Jung's striving toward wholeness both from *Liber secundus* in *The Red Book*. The first one takes place as he is standing guard on a high tower overlooking the valley and encounters the red horseman. Listen to the dialogue as the horseman reveals to Jung his one-sidedness.

> *I am standing on the highest tower of a castle....*
> *I am wearing a green garment. I am the tower*
> *guard. I look out into the distance. I see a red*
> *point out there. It is a horseman in a red coat,*
> *the red horseman.*
> *The Red One: I greet you, man on the high tower.*
> *I saw you from afar, looking and waiting.*
> *I: Who are you?*
> *T.R.: Who am I? You think I am the devil. Do not*
> *pass judgment. Perhaps you can also talk with*
> *me without knowing who I am. What sort of a*
> *superstitious fellow are you, that immediately*
> *you think of the devil?*

I. You make me curious. You seem to be a rare breed...you bring a strange air, something pagan....

T.R. You're an unbelievably ponderous and serious person.

I. You're evasive and don't want to reveal yourself. What are you hiding?

T.R. I hide nothing. What the devil is troubling you? Only Christianity...can make people so ponderous and sullen.

I. I think there are still other things that bespeak seriousness.

T.R. Oh, you mean life. Life doesn't require any seriousness. On the contrary, it's better to dance through life....

I. Perhaps too there is a joy before God that one can call dancing. But I haven't yet found this joy.

T.R. Don't you recognize me brother, I am joy!

I. Could you be joy? Your image fades. Let me take your hand beloved, who are you, who are you? Joy? Was he joy? (The Red Book, 260)

Jung rapidly recognized the Red One as his own devil. But soon he began to realize that this Red One is also his joy, the contrary of his ponderous sullenness. As they talk, the rider's red coat softens like flesh, and Jung's green garment blossoms like a tree. He writes in the commentary that he behaved with his devil as with a real person. That through coming to an understanding with him, Jung accepted some of his joy and his devil accepted some of Jung's seriousness. In Jung's blossoming like a tree in spring, we understand that he is shedding some of his one-sidedness to become more whole. There is a coming together of opposites, a *coniunctio*.

The second dialogue is with his soul, no longer a maiden but a formidable woman, capable of challenging Jung,

197

of showing the headstrong Jung all the scattered parts of himself. Urging Jung to find his own true way. This vision is titled "The Three Prophecies."

> *Wondrous things came nearer. I called my soul and asked her to dive down into the floods, whose distant roaring I could hear.... And thus she plunged into the darkness like a shot, and from the depths she called out:*
>
> *S: "Will you accept what I bring?"*
>
> *I: "I will accept what you give. I do not have the right to judge or to reject."*
>
> *S: "So listen. There is old armor and the rusty gear of our fathers down here, twisted spear heads, broken arrows.... Will you accept all this?"*
>
> *I: "I accept it. You know better, my soul."....*
>
> *S: "I find the treasures of all past cultures, magnificent images of Gods, papyrus rolls... books full of lost wisdom, chants of ancient priests, stories told down the ages."*
>
> *I: "This is an entire world—whose extent I cannot grasp. How can I accept it?"*
>
> *S. "But you wanted to accept everything. You do not know your limits. Can you not limit yourself?*
>
> *I: "I must limit myself. Who could ever grasp such wealth?*
>
> *S: "Be content and cultivate your garden with modesty."*
>
> *I: "I will. I see that it is not worth conquering a larger piece of the immeasurable, but a smaller one instead. A well-tended small garden is better than an ill-tended large garden..."*
>
> *S: "Take shears and prune your trees." (idem, 305-07)*

Jung in the commentary realizes that he must return to the small and the real. To his own modest garden. He has let everything grow without measure. Forests and winding plants. He is covered by endless proliferation. He recognizes his ambition and greed. He asks himself how can he pretend to hold what is not his? His soul agrees: "Beware of knowing what lies beyond yourself.... A knower may know himself. That is his limit." (idem, p. 308)

Jung was in his midlife, and the Soul was telling him to learn to know himself. Who was he? He realizes he has no myth to ground him, no story to live by. Here was someone who had studied the myths of peoples of the past but who himself was without a myth. From his Swiss Protestant upbringing, with his father a pastor, he realizes that he has long ago outlived the Christian myth. It will be his task to elaborate a new myth which will be the synthesis of the confrontation of his ego and the unconscious.

He writes about finding his myth in the Prologue to *Memories, Dreams, Reflections*. "My life is a story of self-realization of the unconscious where everything seeks outward manifestation." The personality seeks to experience itself as a whole. It is a story of individuation, of putting the pieces of his life together. The inner experiences, his dreams and visions. All that constitutes the *prima materia* of his scientific work. Shamdasani points out in his book *The Library of CG Jung* that Jung's years of research, writing, and teaching allowed him to put his discoveries into the scientific language that would give them recognition. That would lead to his final work, *Mysterium Coniunctionis*, written in 1955 and published as volume 14 of *The Collected Works*.

The subtitle of *Mysterium Coniunctionis* is "An Inquiry into the Separation and Synthesis of Psychic Opposites in Alchemy." As we saw in Chapter Six, the alchemists, in looking to turn base metals into gold, were looking to find the spiritual essence of the creation, the *anima mundi*. In psychological terms, they were looking for the archetype of wholeness, the self. Alchemy gave Jung the symbolic language to describe the *coniunctio*, the separation and synthesis of opposites.

Here is the beginning of the first paragraph of this final work.

> *The factors which come together in the coniunctio are conceived as opposites, either confronting one another in enmity or attracting one another in love...moist/dry, cold/warm, upper/lower, spirit-soul/body, heaven/earth, fire/water, bright/dark... good/evil, East/West, living/dead, masculine/ feminine, Sol/Luna. (Mysterium Coniunctionis, par. 1)*

We see Jung now giving words to *Systema munditotius*, the mandala that he painted 45 years earlier. The key to wholeness is the bringing together of opposites. Through the steps of individuation, we become carriers of the opposites. To hold in one hand fire and in the other water, to hold together East and West, good and evil. To no longer project one or the other outside of us. But to carry them together. This is the journey toward wholeness.

It is interesting to see the steps of his journey given physical shape in the construction of his Tower at Bollingen. It was in 1923, still during the years of working on *The Red Book,* that Jung wanted to make a representation in stone of his innermost thoughts. From the start, he knew he would build near water. Originally thinking it would be an African hut crouched on the ground, he found that too primitive and built the first round house, "a suitable dwelling tower."

> *The feeling of repose and renewal that I had in this tower was intense from the start. It represented for me the maternal hearth. But I became increasingly aware that something was lacking. (MDR, 250)*

The journey continued. Something was lacking. Four years later, in 1927, he added the central structure with a tower-like annex. But still he experienced a feeling of incompleteness. And another four years later, in 1931, he extended the tower-like annex in order to have a room in the tower where he could exist for himself alone. It was his retiring room, as he had seen in India, where he would be absolutely alone.

> *In my retiring room I am myself.... Over the years I have done paintings on the walls which have carried me out of time into seclusion, out of the present into timelessness. Thus the second tower became for me a place of spiritual concentration. (idem, 251)*

Jung was still on his quest for wholeness. And once again, four years later, in 1935, feeling he needed a larger space open to the sky and to nature, he added a courtyard and a loggia by the lake. He realized that he had added a fourth element to the threeness of the house. And we see here the squaring of the circle, the wholeness of the number four.

Then after his wife's death in 1955, Jung again felt the need to make still another addition to The Tower. He was that year turning 80. He had reached a serenity that would accompany him until his death six years later. He had become the whole personality that he defined as the goal of individuation. (CW, 9, par. 275). He had become his own self.

He realized that the small central section of the Tower that crouched so low, so hidden, was no longer representative of who he was. He wanted more light, more space, and vaster horizons. He could no longer hide behind the "maternal" and the "spiritual" towers.

> *So in that same year I added an upper storey to this section which represents myself, or my ego-personality. Earlier I would not have been able to do this; I would have regarded it as presumptuous. Now it signified an extension of consciousness achieved in old age. (idem, 251)*

Jung built the house in sections in response to the needs of his personality at the moment. It was a concretization of the individuation process. While he was building each section, he did not consider the long plan. It was only afterwards that he saw how all the parts fitted together, "that a meaningful form had resulted: a symbol of psychic wholeness." (idem, 252)

Certainly it was the wholeness of the structure that imposed itself upon me very recently when I was able to visit the Tower with a small group of Jungian-minded friends, guided by his grandson Hans Hoerni. As it was also the primitiveness. Stone upon stone, put in place by hand, hidden levels and sculptures, a dining table in the middle of the kitchen, steps disappearing upward, the small courtyard enclosed, tower upon tower. Here Jung spent three to four months a year in his old life, without electricity, without running water, and with only wood fires. His grandson remembers arriving as a child and seeing his grandfather and a few friends, wrapped up in overcoats, woolen scarves and gloves, hunched over the table, engrossed in conversation, mindless of the freezing cold. This was the power of the Tower.

The Tower at Bollingen

His two personalities had grown together, the young schoolboy was now the old man, the personality No. 2, who in his visions of *The Red Book* was Philemon, and who came to life again at Bollingen. Here in his Tower, Jung wrote that he was in the midst of his true life. He could take care of himself, tend the fireplace, light the oil lamps, pump the water from the well. Here he could live in harmony with nature, with the world around him.

> *At times I feel as if I am spread out over the landscape and inside things.... Here everything has its history, and mine: here is space for the spaceless kingdom of the world's and the psyche's hinterland. (idem, 252)*

Jung in his old age had found wholeness. Wholeness within himself and within his surroundings. As he wrote,

"Individuation does not shut one out from the world, but gathers the world to one's self." (Vol.8, p.226) Jung was one with the world.

Before moving to another spiritual giant of the 20th century, Thomas Merton, let's ask ourselves where we are in our own search for wholeness.

A writing suggestion:

Take a few moments to remember a moment when you felt at one with yourself? A feeling of wellbeing? Were you near water, in the woods? Were you with a loved one? Write a few lines about the experience.

3. Merton's Search for Wholeness

Let's return now to the Trappist monk Thomas Merton, whom I have included in Chapter One as a journal writer and Chapter Seven as a practitioner of Zen. Merton struggled all his life to bring into harmony his many different personas: the monk, the contemplative, the writer, the poet, the Bohemian, the social activist, the interfaith pioneer, the vulnerable man. Not only was he juggling these different exterior roles, but also he was struggling to find his own interior wholeness. The early death of his mother, his travels with his artist father, his circle of male colleagues at Columbia, the all-male enclosure of a Trappist monastery, left him longing for something hidden deep within himself, the feminine presence.

We can follow Merton's path to wholeness in reading his journals. As he wrote in his notebook, April 14, 1966, "The work of writing can be for me, or very close to, the simple job of being: by creative reflection and awareness to help life itself live in me." (*Learning to Love*, 370) He lived through writing.

Listen here to his words in witnessing a thunderstorm one afternoon in his hermitage, before he had permission to move there permanently.

> *April 15, 1961*
> *Thunderstorm. The first I have sat through in the hermitage. Here you really can watch a storm. White snakes of lightning suddenly stand in the sky and vanish. The valley is clouded with rain as white as milk. All the hills vanish. The thunder cracks and beats. Rain comes flooding down from the roof eaves and the grass looks twice as green as before. (The Intimate Merton, 172)*

He lived the storm, it is as if he himself vanished along with the hills, hearing only the cracking thunder as the rain flooded down. But then the grass turned twice as green. He experienced rebirth.

At the base of Merton's calling as a contemplative was his belief that contemplation is not a compartment of life but rather a way to integrate one's life into a whole. Merton wrote often about the distinction between the false self and the true self, echoing in a way the distinction Jung made between the spirit of this time and the spirit of the depths.

> *The first thing you have to do…is to try to recover your basic natural unity, to reintegrate your compartmentalized being into a coordinated and simple whole and learn to live as a unified human person. This means that you have to bring back together the fragments of your distracted existence so that when you say "I," there is really someone present to support the pronoun you have uttered. (The Inner Experience, 3-4)*

For a life to be lived whole, there has to be this integration. In his essay titled "Final Integration, Toward a 'Monastic Therapy,'" Merton wrote that the man who has attained this wholeness apprehends his life fully from an inner ground that is more universal than the empirical ego. Merton in his last 10 years before his tragic death in 1968 reached out to other traditions, other cultures. His studies of Russian Sophiology, Zen Buddhism, Sufism, indeed of existentialism and Marxism, made him a transcultural monk.

Merton, the integrated monk, had achieved a transcultural maturity. It was this openness to all mankind that made him a peacemaker.

> *The more I am able to affirm others, to say "yes"*
> *to them in myself, by discovering them in myself*
> *and myself in them, the more real I am.... If I*
> *affirm myself as a Catholic merely by denying all*
> *that is Muslim, Jewish, Protestant, Hindu, Buddhist, etc., in the end I will find that there is not*
> *much left for me to affirm as a Catholic: and*
> *certainly no breath of the Spirit with which to*
> *affirm it. (Conjectures of a Guilty Bystander, 144)*

The inner ground that Merton uncovered was the presence of Wisdom—Sophia—the divine presence in the world. She was the unifying thread in Merton's search for wholeness. As he opened to other traditions, Sophia became the key to an all-embracing Christian faith.

Sophia emerged in Merton's life and theology as a presence hidden beyond the surface of everyday reality. She is compassion, unifying humanity. She is what he experienced at Fourth and Walnut Street in Louisville when he realized that he was one with all humankind. She is the beauty of the

Sophia, Drawing by Thomas Merton

natural world that fed his soul. And she is the hand of the nurse that awakened him after his back operation, celebrated in his beautiful prose poem, "Hagia Sophia."

Christopher Pramuk writes in *Sophia, The Hidden Christ of Thomas Merton*, that this poem, "Hagia Sophia," is a hymn of peace celebrating divine Wisdom as the feminine manifestation of God. Here are the opening lines of the first part of this mystical text.

> *There is in all visible things an invisible fecundity, a dimmed light, a meek namelessness, a hidden wholeness. This mysterious Unity and Integrity is Wisdom, the Mother of all.... It rises up in wordless gentleness and flows out to me from the unseen roots of all created being... speaking as Hagia Sophia, speaking as my sister, Wisdom. (Sophia, p. 301)*

A hidden wholeness flowing out from the unseen roots of all created being. The Trappist monk, hidden in Gethsemani, his monastery in Kentucky, was addressing all humanity. It was for this openness to all faiths and peoples that Pope Frances in 2015, we remember, singled him out, one of four great Americans along with Abraham Lincoln, Martin Luther King, and Dorothy Day. "Merton was above all a man of prayer, a thinker who challenged the certitudes of his time...a man of dialogue, a promoter of peace between people and religions."

4. Writing Our Way Toward Wholeness

Both Jung and Merton wrote their way to wholeness. Throughout this book, we have seen writing as a means for self-development, for anchoring inner processes—reflections, meditations, dialogues, dreams—through active imagination. An opportunity to move through change and transitions, to reconnect to the inner flow of life, to release new understanding and vitality. Let's look now at examples from a few contemporary authors who practice writing as a way toward wholeness.

Clarissa Pinkola Estés

Clarissa Pinkola Estés is a contadora, a keeper of old stories in the Latina tradition, a Jungian psychoanalyst and an internationally recognized scholar. In her book, *Women Who Run with the Wolves*, Estés brings forth the ancient wisdom of our ancestors to lead us to the numen, the divine power in the center of the soul where we are one. She does this by collecting and reflecting upon women's stories from "The Wolf Woman" to "The Handless Maiden." Estés shows how stories set the inner life in motion and lead us to our real lives. She writes in the Addendum that her book strives to assist the conscious work of individuation. From her many years of practice with both women and men, she has witnessed the need for psychological and spiritual strength if one wishes to move forward in one's life.

If we read the last story in the book, "The Handless Maiden," we follow step by step the stages of individuation. At the beginning of the miller's daughter's journey to wholeness, we see her total innocence. Her father betrays her by his pact with the devil. She is dismembered, her hands are chopped off. It is now the time of descent as she wanders in the woods, going into the dark, nigredo. There is then the transformation in the underworld, albedo, the new awareness, and the first wedding to the young King, rubedo. The story is not finished. The daughter is sent again into the wildest forest. And finally the second wedding to the King.

Parallel to her journey is the journey of the young King. He too must suffer through seven years of initiation. When he learns that his wife and young son are still alive, he vows to go without eating or drinking and to travel as far as the sky is blue to find them. At last he comes to the inn where the woodspeople are taking care of his wife and their young son. He wakes from a night of sleep and beholds his wife and child. There was great joy in the forest that day.

Estes writes that the two parallel journeys reveal how between the feminine and the masculine, instead of antagonism, there may be profound love, especially when it is rooted in the seeking of the self. She has given us here another version of Jung's confrontation with the unconscious. The tale is not about only one part of our lives, but about the many phases and parts of an entire lifetime. The handless maiden wanders in the forest over and over again, traversing the psychic underworld, until she reunites everything and everyone within her own one self.

Annie Dillard

We return to Annie Dillard, one of our most appreciated contemporary writers, who has figured in Chapter Four concerning the use of metaphor in her collection of essays *Teaching a Stone to Talk*. I refer here to a different book of hers, *For the Time Being*, a nonfiction first-person narrative where several disparate subjects keep recurring in each of seven chapters. Dillard is writing to answer one essential question, How shall one individual live? As the dissimilar scenes and true stories grow familiar to the reader, they make a compound picture of our world. Dillard is putting the pieces together through writing to find the answer.

This personal narrative surveys the panorama of our world. From a natural history of sand to the story of Hasidic thought in Eastern Europe, Dillard asks questions about God and existence. As in a labyrinth she closes in on the answers.

> *This God does not direct the universe, he underlies it…. The more we wake to holiness, the more of it we give birth to, the more we introduce, expand, and multiply it on earth….*
>
> *God decants the universe of time in a stream, and our best hope is, by our own awareness, to step into the stream and serve, empty as flumes, to keep it moving. (For the Time Being, 140, 175)*

To awaken to holiness. To give birth to holiness. To step into the stream of life and serve.

In contemplating life's paradoxes, Dillard finds her answers. In feeling the outstretched hand of a Down's syndrome girl as they walk down from the peak of Mount Tabor, she writes the following.

> *When I started to descend the stairs, a warm hand slid into my hand and grasped it. I turned: An Israeli girl about sixteen years old, a Down's syndrome girl, was holding my hand. I saw the familiar and endearing eyes…. She met my smile and her unbound hair blew in the wind; her cheeks glowed. She held my hand in confidence the length of all the stone stairs. (idem, 191)*

In this short encounter, Dillard describes a *coniunctio*. A coming together, a healthy adult woman and a trusting Down syndrome girl. Dillard reflects upon its meaning. Perhaps, she writes, it takes more time and more people to see the whole of God.

Even Meister Eckhart said, "God needs man."
God needs man to disclose him, complete him,
and fulfill him, Teilhard said…. "Little by little,"
the paleontologist said, "the work is being done."
(idem, 195)

The work of waking to holiness is being done, little by little.

Orhan Pamuk

There is another contemporary author who continues to write toward wholeness, Orhan Pamuk. He figures in Chapter Two of this book as he pursues the image of snow in his novel *Snow*. Here, I turn to his memoir *Istanbul, Memories of a City* in which Pamuk portrays the haunting beauty of his city and identifies with its *hüzün*, its melancholy.

Just as I had lost myself in my imagination to
escape my grandmother's house, I lost myself in
Istanbul. So it was that I finally came to relax and
accept the hüzün that gives Istanbul its grave
beauty, the hüzün that is its fate. (Istanbul, 318)

Pamuk writes that he poured his soul in the city streets of Istanbul, and there it still resides. Istanbul—with its lonely, dark backstreets and ramshackle wooden houses that are disappearing, its chiaroscuro of twilight, the black and white that defines its being—is the hearth that gives back to Pamuk.

If we've lived in a city long enough to have given
our truest and deepest feelings to its prospects,
there comes a time when particular streets,
images and vistas will do the same. (idem, 313)

In identifying with Istanbul, Pamuk is finding his own self.

> *Was this the secret of Istanbul—that beneath its grand history, its living poverty, its sublime landscapes, hid the city's soul inside a fragile web? But here we have come full circle, for anything we say about the city's essence, says more about our own lives and our own states of mind. The city has no centre other than ourselves. (idem, 316)*

Inside this fragile web, he would escape once again into the city's consoling streets, return home, sit down at his table and capture their chemistry on paper. He was going to be a writer. In mirroring his beloved Istanbul, he would bridge the East and West with his words.

Susan Tiberghien

Before concluding this last chapter, I turn to a dream I had during the years of my analysis. It was a terrifying, turbulent dream in which I am trying to make peace between two ancient enemies. I am the housekeeper of one of them, the Giant of Day. Across the way, in another castle, lives the Giant of Night. Once looking out my window before descending for dinner with the Giant of Day, I see the Giant of Night closing his house to leave. I call to him, telling him to come. He and my host have been enemies for too long. I go to open the door. There is a horrendous scene. The two giants go after each other. I try to stop them. The Giant of Day turns on me, pinning me to the ground as if to bite my neck. I awoke in deep fright, powerless to bring the two forces together.

I have written about this dream in my book *Circling to the Center*, including a second dream that followed closely, where a stranger offers me a bouquet of bright yellow flowers, then comes to give me a kiss on the side of my neck where the giant was ready to bite me. Eros was healing me. I was no longer pinned down to the ground. I was free to be with both the Giant of Day and the Giant of Night. It was a *coniunctio, a* coming together of day and night, light and darkness. I kept writing about the experience, journaling to uncover more of its meaning.

Recently, I made it into a folk tale, "The Lady of the Castle." Here is the ending of the tale, just when the lady of the castle goes to open the Giant of Day's castle door to let in the Giant of Night.

> *She went to welcome him. The Giant of Day readied himself. Then swung hard at the Giant of Night, catching him off guard. They locked arms. The fracas thundered down the hallway. The walls shook from their encounter.*
>
> *She pummeled her host with her fists. "Stop this," she shouted. "Let him be" Her eyes blazed. Her hair shone gold.*
>
> *Letting go, the Giant of Day stood back in shock. Tears welled in his eyes.*
>
> *Night had entered his castle.*
>
> *She reached for the hand of her host. Then for the hand of her guest.*
>
> *It was done.*
> *(Offshoots, World Writing from Geneva, 97)*

By continuing to write about my dream, I was growing more aware of each step along the path to wholeness, of opening again and again the door to darkness, realizing that it is a path of a lifetime.

Let's pause for a moment and think about steps we have made. A step to finding a part of ourselves that has been hidden, as Jung did in dialoguing with the Red One. A step to discovering oneness in nature, as Merton did in journaling. A step to finding one's hearth, as Pamuk did in writing *Istanbul*. A step to remembering a dream that points to a *coniunctio*.

A writing exercise:
Remember a step toward wholeness that you have made. Or that you wish to make. Write a few lines about it. A short journal entry to include in your own red book.

Throughout this book, we have been writing toward wholeness. Finding ways to put the parts together, parts of ourselves and parts of the world around us, ways to cultivate the self. We have looked at how to keep our own red books, we have pursued our images, explored our dreams, composed metaphor, seen beauty, practiced alchemy, learned Zen. We have become more conscious of our underlying oneness with all of creation, the rhizome growing underground that never withers. The oneness that has led us to glimpses of the Self, Jung's God-image.

In conclusion, I take two passages from *Memories, Dreams, Reflections,* one from the early pages, the second from the last pages, in this way opening and closing Jung's own journey to wholeness. For the first passage, I turn back to the dream Jung had in his youth that I write about in Chapter Three. The dream appears in the early pages of his autobiography, in the chapter "Student Years."

215

> *It was night in some unknown place and I was
> making slow and painful headway against a
> mighty wind. Dense fog was flying everywhere.
> I had my hands cupped around a tiny light which
> threatened to go out at any moment. Everything
> depended on my keeping this little light alive....
> This little light was my consciousness, the only
> light I have. (MDR, 107-08)*

Jung identifies this light as his consciousness. Each of
us carries this light. Our journey through life is to nourish it,
to nourish our consciousness. To make it more and more
radiant so that it shines forth against the mightiest wind, even
in the darkest of times.

For the second passage, I go to the last pages of the
chapter, "On Life After Death." Jung returns here to this same
little light when he evokes man's feeling for the infinite. It is
with this light—with the consciousness of our wholeness—
that we are able to form a link to the infinite. To the
limitlessness of the unconscious.

> *As far as we can discern, the sole purpose of
> human existence is to kindle a light in the dark-
> ness of mere being. It may even be assumed that
> just as the unconscious affects us, so the increase
> in our consciousness affects the unconscious.
> (idem, 358)*

As we write toward wholeness, we contribute to
humanity's journey to wholeness. Our oneness connects us to
the essence of creation. We touch the infinite. And yes, we
even affect the unconscious. This is our unique destiny.

Bibliography (Books Cited)

Augustine, Saint. *The Confessions*. Translated by Maria Boulding, O.S.B. New York: Vintage Books, Random House, 1998.

Atwood, Margaret. *Negotiating with the Dead: A Writer on Writing*. New York: Cambridge University Press, 2002.

Bosnak, Robert. *The Dream and the Underworld*. New York: Harper & Row, 1979.

Brodsky, Joseph. *Watermark*. New York: Farrar, Straus & Giroux, 1992.

Carson, Anne. *If Not Winter, Fragments of Sappho*. Translated by Anne Carson. New York: Alfred A. Knopf, 2002.

Coelho, Paulo. *The Alchemist*. San Francisco: Harper San Francisco, 1995.

The Dialogues of Plato. Bejamin Jowett, tr. New York: Boni & Liveright, 1927.

Dillard, Annie. *Teaching a Stone to Talk*. New York: Harper Perennial, 1982.

———. *For the Time Being*. New York: Knopf, 1999.

Eckhart, Meister. *Selected Writings*. London: Penguin Books, 1994.

———. *Meister Eckhart, The Essential Sermons, Commentaries, Treatises, and Defense*, Mahwah, NJ: Paulist Press, 1981.

Edinger, Edward F. *The Mysterium Lectures, A Journey through C.G. Jung's Mysterium Coniunctionis*. Toronto, Canada: Inner City Books, 1995.

Epel, Naomi, ed. *Writers Dreaming*. New York: Vintage, 1994.

Estes, Clarissa Pinkola. *Women Who Run with the Wolves*. New York: Ballantine, 1995.

Goldberg, Natalie. *Wild Mind, Living the Writer's Life*. New York: Bantam Books, 1990.

Hamilton, Edith. *Mythology*. New York: Mentor, New American Library, 1969.

Hanh, Thich Nhat. *Cultivating the Mind of Love*. Berkeley, CA: Parallax Press, 1996.

Hildegard of Bingen. *Book of Divine Works with Letters and Songs, Matthew Fox, ed*, Santa Fe: NM: Bear & Company, 1987.

————. *Mystical Visions, translated from Scivias, Know the* Ways, Introduction Matthew Fox. Santa Fe, NM: Bear & Company, 1987.

Hillesum, Etty. *An Interrupted Life and Letters from Westerbork.* New York: Henry Holt, 1996.

Hillman, James. *The Soul's Code.* New York: Random House, 2013.

Hirshfield, Jane. *Women in Praise of the Sacred.* New York: Harpercollins, 1994.

A History of Western Philosophy. W.T. Jones. New York: Harcourt, Brace and Company, 1952.

Hollis, James. *The Archetypal Imagination.* College Station, TX: Texas A&M University Press, 2000.

I Ching or Book of Changes. The Richard Wilhelm Translation, English Rendition Cary F. Baynes, Foreword by C.G.Jung. London: Arkana Penguin Books, 1989.

The Jerusalem Bible. London: Darton, Longman & Todd, 1974.

Johnson, Robert. *We, Understanding the Psychology of Romantic Love.* San Francisco, CA: Harper San Francisco, 1983.

Julian of Norwich. *Revelations of Divine Love.* Translated by Clifton Wolters. London: Penguin Books, 1966. Also, Translated by Elizabeth Spearing. London: Penguin Books, 1998.

Jung, C.G. *Aion, Researches into the Phenomenology of the Self, Volume 9.* Princeton NJ: Princeton University Press, 1969.

————. *Answer to Job, The Portable Jung,* New York: Penguin Books, 1976.

————. *Man and His Symbols.* London: Picador, 1964.

————. *Memories, Dreams, Reflections.* London: Fontana Paperbacks, 1989.

————. *Mysterium Coniunctionis.* Princeton, NJ: Princeton University Press, 1979.

————. *On the Nature of the Psyche*, Volume 8: Princeton, NJ: Princeton University Press, 1960.

————. *Synchronicity, Foreword Sonu Shamdasani.* Princeton, NJ: Princeton University Press, 2010.

————. *The Red Book.* New York: W.W. Norton & Company, 2009.

Lao Tzu. *Tao Te Ching.* Translated by Gia-Fu Feng and Jane English. New York: Vintage Books, 1989.

Lü Yen. *The Secret of the Golden Flower, Translator Richard Wilhelm, Commentary C.G. Jung.* New York: London: A Harvest/HBJ Book, 1962.

Merton, Thomas. *A Vow of Conversation, Journals 1964-65.* New York: Farrar, Straus, Giroux, 1988.

———. *Dancing in the Water of Life, Journals, Volume V.* San Francisco CA: HarperSanFrancisco, 1997.

———. *Love and Living.* San Diego, New York, London, Harcourt, Inc., 1979.

———. *The Seven Storey Mountain.* 50th Anniversary Issue. New York: Harcourt Brace & Company, 1998.

———. *The Asian Journal of Thomas Merton.* New York: New Directions, 1973.

———. *The Way of Chuang Tzu.* New York: New Directions, 1969.

———. *Zen and the Birds of Appetite.* New York: New Directions, 1968.

Montaldo, Jonathan & Hart, Patrick. *The Intimate Merton.* San Francisco: HarperSanFrancisco, 1999.

Moore, Dinty W. *The Mindful Writer.* Boston, MA: Wisdom Publications, 2012.

Muhammed, Abdullah ibn. *The Koran,* John Medow Rodwell, tr. New York, Bantam/Dell, 2004.

O'Donohue, John. *Beauty, the Invisible Embrace.* New York: HarperCollins Perennial Edition, 2005.

Ovid. *Metamorphoses,* London: Penguin Books, 1955.

Pamuk, Orhan. *Snow.* London: Faber and Faber, 2004.

———. *Istanbul, Memories of a City.* London: Faber and Faber, 2005.

Pramuk, Christopher. *Sophia, The Hidden Christ of Thomas Merton.* Collegeville, Minnesota: Liturgical Press, 2009.

Rilke, Rainer Maria. *Letters to a Young Poet.* New York: Norton, 1962.

———. *Duino Elegies.* Translated by David Oswald. Einsiedeln: Daimon Verlag, 1992.

Shakespeare, William. *Complete Works of Shakespeare,* Scott, Foresman & Co. New York 1951.

Shamdasani, Sonu. *C.G. Jung, A Biography in Books.* New York: W.W. Norton and Company, 2012.

Stein, Murray. *Minding the Self.* London and New York: Routledge, 2014.

———. *Jung's Map of the Soul.* Chicago, IL: Open Court, 1998.

Suzuki, D.T. *Zen Buddhism, Selected Writings of DT Suzuki,* New York: Image Books, Doubleday, 1996.

Suzuki, Shunryu. *Zen Mind, Beginner's Mind.* New York & Tokyo: Weatherhill, 1991.

Tiberghien, Susan M. *Circling to the Center, One Woman's Encounter with Silent Prayer.* Mahwah, NJ: Paulist Press, 2000.

———. *Footsteps, In Love with a Frenchman.* New York: Red Lotus Studio Press, 2015.

———. *Looking for Gold, A Year in Jungian Analysis.* Second Edition, Einsiedeln, Switzerland: Daimon Verlag, 2007.

———. *One Year to a Writing Life, Twelve Lessons to Deepen Every Writer's Art and Craft.* Cambridge, MA: Da Capo Press, Lifelong Books, 2007.

———. *Side by Side, Writing Your Love Story.* New York: Red Lotus Studio Press, 2015.

Von Franz, Marie-Louise. *Alchemy.* Toronto: Inner City Books, 1980.

Weil, Simone. *Waiting for God.* New York: Perennial Library, Harper & Row, 1992.

Williams, Terry Tempest. *Finding Beauty in a Broken World.* New York: Pantheon Books, 2008.

———. *When Women Were Birds.* Sarah Crichton Books, Ferrar, Strauss and Giroux, 2012.

Woodman, Marion. *Bone, Dying into Life.* New York: Viking Penguin. 2000.

Wu, C.H. *The Golden Age of Zen.* New York, London: Image Books Doubleday, 1996.

Credits

Grateful acknowledgment is made for excerpts from the following books.

From *Negotiating with the Dead*, by Margaret Atwood, Cambridge University Press. With permission of Cambridge University Press.

From *The Confessions*, by Saint Augustine, Random House. With permission of Penguin Random House.

From *Watermark*, by Joseph Brodsky, Farrar, Straus & Giroux.

From *If Not Winter, Fragments of Sappho,* by Anne Carson (Translator), Alfred A. Knopf.

From *The Alchemist*, by Paulo Coehlo, HarperCollins Publishers.

From *For the Time Being,* by Annie Dillard, Knopf. With permission of PenguinRandomHouse and permission of Russell & Volkening.

From *Teaching a Stone to Talk: Expeditions and Encounters* by Annie Dillard. Copyright © 1982 by Annie Dillard. Reprinted by permission of HarperCollins Publishers and permission of Russell & Volkening.

From *Writers Dreaming*, by Naomi Epel, Vintage Books. With permission of Naomi Epel.

From *Wild Mind*, by Natalie Goldberg, Bantam Books. With permission of PenguinRandomHouse. Also published by Rider. Reproduced by permission of the Random House Group LTD © 1991.

From *Cultivating the Mind of Love*, Thich Nhat Hahn, Parallax Press. With permission of Parallax Press, Berkeley, California.

From *Book of Divine Works,* by Hildegard von Bingen, Bear & Company Publishing.

From *An Interrupted Life*, The Diaries 1941-1943 *and Letters from Westerbork* by Etty Hillesum. *An Interrupted Life* English language translation copyright © 1983 by Jonathan Cape Ltd. Used by permission of Henry Holt and Company. All rights reserved.

Index

Alchemy 14, 40, 133-137, 139-
143, 145, 146, 148, 149, 152,
156, 159, 193, 200, 215, 221

Anima / Animus 22, 135, 193,
200

Albedo 133, 146, 151, 153

Angelou, Maya 79

Archetype 50, 68, 135, 189, 200

Aristophanes 74, 190, 191

Aristotle 22, 86, 136

Asclepius 64

Atwood, Margaret 134, 150, 151,
156, 217

Augustine, Saint Augustine 112

Baucis 98, 143

Beauty 3, 14, 22, 27, 29, 34, 58,
68, 89, 95, 109-120, 122, 123,
125-132, 208, 212, 215, 220,
221

Blake 109

Bollingen, The Tower 6, 96, 118,
174, 187, 200, 202, 203

Bosnak, Robert 67, 217

Brodsky, Joseph 134, 152, 153,
156, 217

Buddha 64, 162, 172, 178, 179,
182-184

Cathedral / Chapel / Church 5,
15, 48, 65, 96, 100, 101, 108,
115, 124, 130, 131, 151, 152,
154

Chuang Tzu 6, 63, 160, 170,
171, 219

Coelho, Paulo 134, 151, 152, 217

Confucianism 160, 168

Coniunctio 120, 137, 193, 194,
198, 200, 211, 214, 215, 217,
219

Conscious/Consciousness 9, 11,
13, 16, 17, 33, 39-41, 73, 74,
78, 133, 146, 149, 152, 156,
163, 166, 193, 209, 215

Cora / Persephone 123, 125

Descartes 66, 140

Desert 43, 44, 97, 98, 151, 152,
189, 193

Dillard, Annie 85, 101-103, 107,
188, 210, 211, 217

For the Time Being 210, 211,
217

Teaching a Stone to Talk 101,
102, 210, 217

Dorn, Gerhard 139

Dreams 3, 8, 9, 11, 13-16, 19,
23, 25-27, 39, 40, 45, 53, 61-
68, 70, 71-83, 85, 94, 95, 99,
104, 105, 107, 117-119, 133,
134, 139, 145, 151, 152, 173,
182, 199, 209, 213-215, 217,
219, 220

Dreamwork 71-74

Eckhart, Meister 23, 39, 142, 179, 185, 212, 217

Edinger, Edward, 40

Ego 61, 146, 148, 168, 193, 194, 199, 202, 206

Elijah 16, 98, 99, 100, 164, 193

Epel, Naomi 77, 78, 81, 82

Eros 21, 98, 99, 193, 194, 214

Estés, Clarissa Pinkola 188, 209, 217

Faust 39, 65, 72, 73

Francis of Assisi 65, 113, 224

Freud, Sigmund 11, 13, 16, 17, 65, 66, 96, 97, 192

Gethsemani Monastery 171, 208

Gilgamesh 62, 88, 98, 150, 164

Ginkgo Tree 6, 169, 170, 185

Gnosticism 143, 145

God 9, 12, 19-21, 29, 32, 44, 62-65, 77, 88, 90, 91, 93, 95-100, 109, 110, 112, 113, 116, 122, 123, 125, 128, 129, 143, 144, 146, 155, 160, 165, 184, 189-192, 194, 197, 198, 208, 211, 212, 215, 221

Goldberg, Natalie 159, 180, 217

Golden Flower 41, 133, 137, 141, 142, 146, 154-157, 159, 163, 165, 166, 219, 220

Hanh, Thich Nhat 159, 178-180, 218

Hart, Patrick 31, 220

Hestia 187, 189

Hildegard of Bingen 5, 22, 23, 51, 91, 92, 113

Hillesum, Etty 16, 27, 28, 33, 134, 149, 218

Hillman, James 24, 72, 218

Hinshaw, Robert 6, 7, 196

Hirshfield, Jane 222

Hollis, James 87, 219

I Ching 167

Images 3, 5, 6, 11, 15, 16, 18, 20, 21, 23, 24, 26, 34, 35, 37-45, 47, 48, 49-51, 53-59, 65, 66, 70, 71, 73-78, 80-82, 89, 93, 94, 96-98, 100, 101, 107, 108, 119, 120, 124-126, 128-131, 133, 141, 145, 146, 149, 153, 185, 192, 193, 196-198, 212, 213, 215, 221

Imagination, Active 3, 12, 37, 38, 39, 40, 42, 43, 45, 47, 49, 54, 59, 70, 99, 165, 209

Inanna 109-111

Individuation 30, 96, 124, 125, 133, 140, 142, 149, 166, 187, 193, 194, 199, 200, 202, 204, 209

Izdubar 16, 62, 88, 98, 100, 159, 163, 164, 165

Jesus 12, 90

Johnson, Robert 66, 218

Julian of Norwich 187, 191, 192

Jung, C.G. 1, 5-8, 10-21, 23, 24, 26, 27, 30, 31, 33, 35, 37-46, 48, 50-54, 59, 61, 62, 65-70, 75, 83, 85, 88, 93-101, 107-

109, 118-122, 124, 125, 127, 129, 130, 132-135, 137, 139-150, 156, 168, 173, 182, 187, 195, 217-220

Aion 146, 218

Black Books 10, 17, 31, 40, 42

Dialogues 13, 47, 98, 101, 190, 196, 209, 217

Dreams 8, 13, 14, 16, 26, 27, 85, 94, 95, 107, 118, 133, 139, 182, 199, 215, 219

Letters 100, 174

Memories, Dreams, Reflections 8, 13-15, 26, 27, 85, 94, 95, 107, 118, 139, 182, 215, 219

My Soul Approached Me 5, 51, 52

Mysterium Coniunctionis 17, 40, 200, 217, 219

Night Sinks Blue 5, 120, 121

On the Nature of the Psyche 219

Philosopher's Stone, The 6, 100, 135, 139, 140, 146, 149, 157

Psychology and Alchemy 137, 140

Red Book, The 5, 6, 8, 10, 11, 13-18, 23, 26, 31, 35, 37, 38, 40, 42, 44, 48, 51, 52, 62, 68, 69, 85, 88, 94, 97-100, 107, 108, 119-121, 124, 125, 131, 133, 141-148, 150,

159, 163, 165, 187, 193-197, 200, 201, 203, 215, 219

Systema munditotius 6, 51, 193, 196, 200

Window to Eternity 5, 61, 67, 69, 70

Keller 7, 38, 39, 45, 72-74, 77

King, Stephen 79, 80

Koan 162, 185

Labyrinth 5, 122-127, 130, 145, 211

Lao Tsu 137, 160, 187, 189, 190, 219

Logos 98, 99, 193, 194

Magic 120, 140, 144, 155, 156

Mandala 22, 37, 50, 51, 53, 54, 56, 70, 91, 93, 96, 100, 120, 127, 141, 154, 189, 193, 194, 196, 200

Merton, Thomas 6, 8, 16, 30-33, 109, 115, 116, 170-173, 178, 179, 187, 188, 204-210, 215, 219, 220

Conjectures of a Guilty Bystander 206

Dancing in the Water of Life 31, 32, 219

Hagia Sophia 208

Inner Experience, The 199, 206

Intimate Merton, The 205, 220

Learning to Love 205

Seven Story Mountain 30

Vow of Conversation, A 32, 33, 116, 172, 219

Way of Chuang Tzu, The 171, 219

Zen, Birds of Appetite 172, 185, 219

Metaphor 3, 13, 85-91, 93, 94, 96, 97, 98, 100-108, 110, 122, 135, 210, 215

Montaldo, Jonathan 31, 220

Moore, Dinty W. 159, 181, 182, 220

Morgan, Christiana 15, 24, 35, 38, 100, 130

Muhammad 65, 90

Myth 12, 23, 61, 74, 87, 89, 96, 98, 123, 143, 165, 190, 199

Nigredo 133, 146, 149, 151, 153, 156

O'Donohue 109, 116, 117

Ovid 98, 143, 220

Pamuk, Orhan 37, 55, 56, 188, 212, 213, 215, 220

   Snow 55, 56, 212, 220

   Istanbul 55, 212, 213, 215, 220

Philemon 16, 98, 101, 143, 144, 156, 196, 203

Plato 22, 89, 90, 111, 187, 190, 217

   Phaedrus 22, 111

   Republic, The 89, 90

   Symposium 111, 190

Polonnaruwa, Sri Lanka 116, 172, 173

Pramuk, Christopher 208, 220

Price, Reynold 80, 81

Psyche 10-12, 21, 39, 40, 61, 66, 73, 124, 148, 166, 167, 193, 204, 219

Quran 65, 90, 220

Red Knight, the 16, 98, 100, 164

Rhizome 5, 94-96, 215

Rilke, Rainer Maria 26, 39, 114, 150, 220

   Letters to a Young Poet 26, 114, 220

   Duino Elegies 115, 220

Rubedo 133, 146, 148, 151, 152, 153

Salome 16, 98-100, 164, 193

Sappho 111

Satori 161-163, 166, 168, 173

Secret of the Golden Flower 41, 133, 137, 141, 142, 156, 157, 159, 163, 165, 166, 219

Self 3, 13, 14, 23, 25, 29-31, 41, 43, 44, 67, 68, 94, 96, 97, 100, 120, 125, 129, 133, 135, 137, 140, 146, 148, 149, 166, 167, 176, 184, 187, 193, 194, 200, 202, 204, 205, 210, 213, 215, 218, 220

Senior (Ibn Umail) 139

Serpent 16, 98, 100, 164, 194

Shadow 27, 89, 90, 146, 149, 172

Shakespeare 86, 93, 220

Shamdasani, Sonu 6, 8, 17, 42, 125, 142, 149, 159, 199, 219
Siddhartha Gautama 160, 162
Simile 87, 94, 102
Socrates 22, 89, 109, 111, 190
Song of Songs, The 88
Sophia 6, 188, 194, 206-208, 220
Soul 3, 5, 10-13, 15, 16-24, 26-28, 30-33, 35, 37-39, 43, 44, 51, 52, 54, 61, 85, 88, 89, 97, 98, 100, 109, 111, 119, 122, 131, 132, 134, 135, 137, 139, 140, 142, 146, 150, 152, 163, 166, 173, 179, 193, 198-200, 208-210, 212, 213, 218, 220
Spirit of the Depths 18-20, 43, 48, 97, 192, 193
Spirit of the Times 18, 19, 20, 43, 48, 97, 192, 193
Stein, Murray 9, 12, 94, 142, 220
    Minding the Self 94, 220
    Jung's Map of the Soul 12, 142, 220
St. John of the Cross 134, 149
Styron, William 78, 82
Suzuki, D.T. 159, 162, 163, 168, 175, 221
Suzuki, Shunryu 159, 162, 176, 177, 192, 221
Synchronicity 25, 105, 142, 167, 219
Synesius 64, 65
Taoism, 160, 168, 188
Tiberghien, Susan 1, 2, 5, 6, 9, 12, 104, 129, 153, 213, 221

Cinquefoil 6, 153, 154, 156
Circling to the Center 153-155, 214, 221
Crack in the Water Jug 5, 104, 106
Dogwood Blossom 5, 53, 54, 115, 116
Double Buttercup 6, 155
Footsteps 106, 107, 221
Green Frog 5, 71, 76
Green Ivy 5, 130, 131
Journal Entries 19, 35, 108
Looking for Gold 7, 14, 45, 71, 73, 76, 104, 105, 196, 221
Mandalas 37, 50, 51, 53, 54, 70, 127
One Year to a Writing Life 25, 184, 221
Side by Side 129, 130, 221
Transcendent Function 46
Tree 5, 6, 27, 28, 29, 39, 42, 44-47, 49, 53, 67, 68, 70, 76, 80, 89, 91, 92, 95, 98, 101, 115, 117, 120, 151, 152, 162, 167, 169, 170, 174, 179, 185, 188, 192, 197-199
Unconscious 9, 11, 13, 15, 21, 38-43, 48, 50, 61, 66, 67, 73-77, 83, 96, 97, 100, 101, 106, 108, 125, 133, 134, 140, 141, 145, 146, 148, 153, 163, 166, 182, 185, 187, 193, 196, 199, 210, 216

Von Franz, Marie-Louise 135, 136, 139, 221

Weil, Simone 109, 122, 123, 125, 127, 221

Wholeness 1, 3, 7-15, 24, 25, 27, 28, 30, 32, 33, 35, 37, 47, 50, 51, 54, 59, 61, 94, 96, 108, 135, 149, 159, 166, 187-194, 196, 200-202, 204, 206, 208, 209, 212, 215, 216

Wilhelm, Richard 137, 141, 142, 218-220

Williams, Terry Tempest 37, 56-58, 110, 126, 127, 221
  When Women Were Birds 56-58, 221
  Finding Beauty in a Broken World 126, 127, 221

Woodman, Marion 110, 127-129

Wu, John C.H. 168-173, 221

Zen 3, 14, 74, 159, 160-163, 167-169, 171-173, 175-178, 180, 181, 184, 185, 188, 192, 204, 206, 215, 219, 221

Zosimos 139, 140

About the Author

Susan Tiberghien, an American writer living in Geneva, Switzerland, holds a BA in Literature and Philosophy and did graduate work at Grenoble University, France and the CG Jung Institute, Kusnacht, Switzerland.

She has published four memoirs: *Looking for Gold, A Year in Jungian Analysis; Circling to the Center, An Invitation to Silent Prayer; Side by Side: Writing Your Love Story; Footsteps: In Love with a Frenchman*, and the writing handbook, *One Year to a Writing Life, Twelve Lessons to Deepen Every Writer's Art and Craft*, along with numerous essays in journals and anthologies on both sides of the Atlantic.

Tiberghien has been teaching Jungian inspired writing workshops for over twenty years at C.G. Jung Societies, at the International Women's Writing Guild, and at writers' centers and conferences in the States and in Europe. She is an active member of International PEN, a founding member of the International Writers Residence at Lavigny, Switzerland, and the director of the Geneva Writers' Group, an association of over 240 English-language writers, which she founded in 1993.

Mother of six children and sixteen grandchildren, she lives with her husband in Geneva, Switzerland.

www.susantiberghien.com

CPSIA information can be obtained
at www.ICGtesting.com
Printed in the USA
FSHW011821070719
59778FS